THE PASSION OF
BRADLEY MANNING

M

THE PASSION OF
BRADLEY MANNING

Chase Madar

VERSO
London • New York

First published by OR Books, New York and London 2012
This updated edition published by Verso 2013
© Chase Madar 2013
All rights reserved

The moral rights of the author have been asserted

1 3 5 7 9 10 8 6 4 2

Verso
UK: 6 Meard Street, London W1F 0EG
US: 20 Jay Street, Suite 1010, Brooklyn, NY 11201

www.versobooks.com

Verso is the imprint of New Left Books

ISBN-13: 978-1-78168-069-8

British Library Cataloguing in Publication Data
A catalogue record for this book is available from the British Library

Library of Congress Cataloging-in-Publication Data
A catalog record for this book is available from the Library of Congress

Typeset by MJ Gavan, Truro, Cornwall
Printed by in the US by Maple Vail

TABLE OF CONTENTS

1

A MEDAL FOR BRADLEY MANNING

(02:05:12 AM) **bradass87:** its almost bookworthy in itself, how this played

Bradley Manning deserves the Presidential Medal of Freedom.

If the 24-year-old Army private from Crescent, Oklahoma, did supply Wikileaks with its choicest material—the Iraq War logs, the Afghan War logs, and the State Department cables—then he surely deserves some important national honor instead of the military prison cell where he presently awaits court martial.

Charged under the Espionage Act of 1917 and with aiding the enemy, Bradley Manning faces life in prison. He has put his sanity and his freedom on the line so that Americans might know what their government has done—and is doing—all over the world. Knowing what our government is doing abroad is not a special privilege for statesmen, spies and insider journalists, it is the right and responsibility of all citizens. Manning has blown the whistle on criminal violations of American military and international law. He has exposed our government's pathological over-classification of important public documents.

There are at least five reasons why Manning, if he did what the government accuses him of doing, deserves that medal.

1. For Giving Our Foreign Policy Elite the Public Supervision It So Badly Needs

In the past ten years, American statecraft has moved from one catastrophe to another, laying waste to other nations while never failing to damage its own national interests. One lauded study finds that the past decade's wars have resulted in the deaths of at least 174,000 civilians, 31,741 Allied military personnel (including 8,351 US soldiers and military contractors) and have cost the US treasury upwards of $3.7 trillion.[1]

Although downsizing our entire foreign policy establishment is not an option, the website Wikileaks has at least brought public scrutiny to bear on our self-destructive statesmen and -women. No one should be more grateful for these revelations than Americans, whose government has deceived us with such horrible consequences.

Consider our invasion of Iraq, a war based on willful distortions, government secrecy, and the complaisant failure of our major media to ask the important questions. But what if someone like Bradley Manning had provided the press with the necessary government documents, which would have made so much self-evident in the months before the war began?

Thanks to Manning's alleged disclosures, we have a sense of what transpired in Iraq and Afghanistan. We have a far clearer image of how Washington operates in the world. Thanks to those revelations we now know just how our government leaned on the Vatican to quell opposition to the Iraq War. We now know how Washington pressured the German government to block the prosecution of CIA agents who kidnapped an innocent man, Khaled El-Masri, while he was on vacation.[2] We know how our State Department lobbied hard to prevent a minimum wage increase in Haiti, the hemisphere's poorest nation.[3] It is all to our benefit that more whistleblowers make themselves heard. A foreign policy based on secrets and spin has manifestly failed us. In a democracy, statecraft cannot function if it is shrouded in secrecy. For bringing us the truth, for breaking the seal on that self-protective policy of secrecy, Bradley Manning deserves the Presidential Medal of Freedom.

2. For Exposing the Pathological Over-Classification of America's Public Documents

"Secrecy is for losers," as the late Senator and United Nations Ambassador Daniel Patrick Moynihan used to say.[4] If this is indeed the case, it would be hard to find a bigger loser than the US government. When Moynihan, a conservative Democrat who served as Nixon's UN envoy, wrote those words in 1991, the US was classifying upwards of six million documents a year. Today that figure has risen by an order of magnitude, with Washington classifying some ninety-two million documents in 2011.[5]

Government secrecy, especially in the domain of foreign affairs, has become pathological. In June 2011, the National Security Agency declassified documents from 1809, while the Department of Defense[6] declassified the Pentagon Papers, publicly available in book form these last four decades. Our government is only now finishing its declassification of documents relating to World War I.

This would be ridiculous if it weren't tragic. Ask the historians. Barton J. Bernstein, professor emeritus of history at Stanford University and a founder of its international relations program, describes the government's classification of foreign-policy documents as "bizarre, arbitrary, and nonsensical." George Herring, professor emeritus at the University of Kentucky and author of the encyclopedic *From Colony to Superpower: A History of US Foreign Policy*, has chronicled how his delight at being appointed to a CIA advisory panel on declassification turned to disgust once he realized that he was being used as window dressing by an agency with no intention of opening its records, no matter how important or how old, to public scrutiny.[7]

The people of a democratic state ignore such signs at their risk. If a society like ours doesn't know its own history, it becomes the great power equivalent of a wandering amnesiac, not knowing what it did yesterday or where it will end up tomorrow. Right now, classification is the disease of Washington, secrecy its mania, and dementia its end point. This is not just the diagnosis made by groups like the ACLU and Wikileaks; J. William Leonard, career federal civil servant and director of the Information Security Oversight Office from 2002 to 2007, has recently called for sanctions against officials who gratuitously classify government documents.[8]

President Obama came into office promising a "sunshine" policy for his administration while singing the praises of whistleblowers. Instead, he has launched the fiercest campaign against whistleblowers the republic has ever seen, and dragged our foreign policy deeper into the shadows. Challenging the classification of each tightly guarded document is impossible. No organization has the resources to fight this fight, nor would they be likely to win right now. Absent a radical change in our government's diplomatic and military bureaucracies, massive over-classification will only continue.

If we hope to know what our government is so busily doing all over the world, massive leaks from insider whistleblowers are, like it or not, the only recourse. Our whistleblower protection laws urgently need to catch up to this state of affairs, and though we are hardly there yet, Bradley Manning helped take us part of the way. He did what Barack Obama swore he would do on coming into office. For striking a blow against our government's fanatical and counterproductive habit of secrecy, Bradley Manning deserves not punishment but the Presidential Medal of Freedom.

3. For Doing More Than Any American Alive to Advance the Cause of Freedom Abroad

Wasn't it official policy to spread democracy around the world—especially to the Middle East—and to extend our freedom to others, as all recent American presidents have soaringly proclaimed?

Things haven't exactly turned out that way. On the one hand, plans to remake the Middle East have swirled into violent chaos at great cost in human life. On the other, America has lavished financial and military support on autocrats in Egypt, Bahrain, Saudi Arabia and Yemen—and on ethnic cleansing in occupied Palestine. Both sets of policies, both backed by broad bipartisan consensus, have made a joke of Washington's "Freedom Agenda."

Against this backdrop stands the glowing contribution of Bradley Manning to freedom and justice around the world. Thanks to his alleged leaks, the people of Libya know about Muammar Qaddaffi's cozy evening with Senator John McCain, and the latter's eagerness to supply the dictator with American-made armaments.[9] The people of Bahrain know about their vicious ruler's praise for the Pentagon's military training center in Manama, not to mention his fond memories of his tutelage at the Army Command and General Staff College in Fort Leavenworth, where Manning was for months imprisoned.[10] And the people of Tunisia had confirmed by a classified State Department cable what most already suspected: the thuggish and thoroughgoing corruption of the ruling Ben-Ali family.[11]

Did Wikileaks "cause" the Arab Spring, as some have implied? Of course not. From Tunisia to Egypt to Yemen to Bahrain to Syria and beyond, these societies were smoldering with long-held grievances against stifling authoritarian rule, often backed by Washington. The contributions of Wikileaks are small, but they are not insignificant. "You cannot get away from Wikileaks in any account of the Tunisian uprising," says Larbi Sadiki, a Tunisian-born political scientist. "You need to see the clear record of injustice and corruption inflicted by a cabal of powerful men."[12]

Even if US policy has often been on the wrong side of things, we should be proud that at least one American—Bradley Manning—was on the right side and made his own modest but significant contribution to the freedom of foreign nations. For this he deserves the Presidential Medal of Freedom.

4. For Performing His Duties in Exemplary Fashion

What are a soldier's duties when faced with torture? In 2005, General Peter Pace, Chairman of the Joint Chiefs of Staff, told reporters: "It is absolutely the responsibility of every US service member [in Iraq], if they see inhumane treatment being conducted, to try to stop it."[13] This, according to the highest-ranking soldier in the land, was the obligation of every US service member in Operation Iraqi Freedom. It is a duty that Pfc. Manning has fulfilled.

Bradley Manning enlisted in the US Army to make a difference. He enlisted in 2007, in part out of family tradition (his father was a Naval intelligence officer), in part out of hopes of a military-funded university education after his deployment, and in large part out of patriotic service. "He was basically really into America," says a hometown friend. "He was proud of our successes as a country. He valued our freedom, but probably our economic freedom the most. I think he saw the US as a force for good in the world."[14]

When Bradley Manning deployed to Iraq in October 2009, he thought that he'd be helping the Iraqi people build a free society after the long nightmare of Saddam Hussein. He thought Operation Iraqi Freedom was supposed to have something to do with Iraqi Freedom, especially freedom from state torture.

He soon found himself helping the Iraqi authorities detain civilians for distributing "anti-Iraqi literature"—which turned out to be an investigative report into financial corruption in their own government entitled "Where Does The Money Go?" The penalty for this "crime" in Iraq was not a slap on the wrist. Imprisonment and torture, as well as systematic abuse of prisoners, are widespread in the new Iraq. From the military's own Sigacts (Significant Actions) reports, we have a multitude of credible accounts of Iraqi police and soldiers shooting prisoners, beating them to death, pulling out fingernails or teeth, cutting off fingers, burning with acid, torturing with electric shocks or the use of suffocation, and various kinds of sexual abuse including sodomy with gun barrels and forcing prisoners to perform sexual acts on guards and each other.

Manning had more than adequate reason to be concerned about handing over Iraqi citizens for likely torture simply for producing pamphlets about corruption. Like any good soldier, Manning immediately took these concerns up the chain of command. And how did his superiors respond? According to Manning, his commanding officer told him to "shut up" and get back to rounding up more prisoners for the Iraqi Federal Police to treat however they cared to.[15] And this is no surprise: in the course of its eight-year occupation, the American military handed over thousands of prisoners to the Iraqi authorities, knowing full well what would happen to many of them.

It is unclear—and contested—whether the US military had a legal obligation to carry out General Pace's public exhortation to prevent torture by local authorities. Secretary of Defense Donald Rumsfeld certainly disagreed with his top general's exhortation, and secretly issued Fragmentary Order 242, which made noninterference with Iraqi torture official US policy.[16] The laws of armed conflict generally impose a light burden on occupying armies, though they do impose ample restrictions on the people being occupied, especially insurgents and "unprivileged non-uniformed combatants"—formerly referred to as "savages" in the common discourse of international law. Though it may seem outrageous, most interpreters of the Geneva Conventions would agree, however reluctantly, that it was strictly lawful for occupying US military to hand over local citizens, even nonviolent citizen activists, to the Iraqi authorities where they faced a decent likelihood torture.

Refusing to interfere with torture was probably lawful. But was it honorable?

Bradley Manning may not have always been a model soldier, but if we are to believe the accusations, his bravery was remarkable and he was a true believer in his mission. He believed Operation Iraqi Freedom had something to do with planting and nurturing Iraqi freedom, especially that most fundamental liberty, freedom from torture and arbitrary detention.

Pfc. Manning acted in accordance with his belief in the mission to spread freedom in Iraq. By blowing the whistle on programmatic institutional complicity with torture, Bradley Manning made a moral choice that honored his uniform and his country. For the example he has set, he fully deserves the Presidential Medal of Freedom.

5. For Upholding an American Tradition of Transparency in Statecraft

Bradley Manning is only the latest in a long line of whistleblowers in and out of uniform who have risked everything to put our country back on the right path.

Take Daniel Ellsberg, leaker of the Pentagon Papers, a Pentagon-commissioned secret history of the Vietnam War and the official lies and distortions that the government used to sell it. Many of the documents it included were classed at a much higher security clearance than anything Bradley Manning is accused of releasing—and yet Ellsberg was not convicted of a single crime, and became a national hero.

Given the era when all this went down, it's forgivable to assume that Ellsberg must have been a hippie who somehow sneaked into the Pentagon archives, beads and patchouli trailing behind. What many no longer realize is that Ellsberg had been a model US Marine. First in his class at officer training school at Quantico, he deferred graduate school at Harvard to remain on active duty during the Suez crisis of 1956. Ellsberg saw his high-risk exposure of the disastrous and deceitful nature of the Vietnam War as fully consonant with his long career of patriotic service in and out of uniform.

And Ellsberg is hardly alone. Lt. Colonel (ret.) Darrel Vandeveld, former lead prosecutor of a child soldier at Guantánamo, quit in a crisis of conscience. And Thomas Drake, formerly of the National Security Agency: his exposure of waste and severe abuse of wiretapping powers earned him the relentless prosecution of the Obama Justice Department. And former infantryman Ethan McCord, who rescued children from the van shot up by the Apache gunship in the Collateral Murder video, has since condemned the lax and illegal rules of engagement he received from his superiors in Iraq and praised Bradley Manning as a hero.

Transparency in statecraft was not invented by Julian Assange. It is a longstanding American tradition that dates back to the first years of the republic. A 1960 Congressional Committee on Government Operations report caught the same spirit: "Secrecy—the first refuge of incompetents—must be at a bare minimum in a democratic society... Those elected or appointed to positions of executive authority must recognize that government, in a democracy, cannot be wiser than the people." John F. Kennedy made the same point in 1961: "The very word 'secrecy' is repugnant in a free and open society." Hugo Black, great Alabama justice of the twentieth-century Supreme Court, had this to say: "The guarding of military and diplomatic secrets at the expense of informed representative government provides no real security for our Republic." And the first of World War I-era president Woodrow Wilson's Fourteen Points couldn't have been more explicit: "Open covenants of peace, openly arrived at, after which there shall be no private international understandings of any kind but diplomacy shall proceed always frankly and in the public view."

We need to know what our government's commitments are. Our foreign policy elites have clearly demonstrated they cannot be left to their own devices. Based on the last decade of carnage and folly, without public debate—and aggressive media investigations—we have every reason to expect our foreign affairs to keep playing out as Madison predicted.

Many of the principle players in this tragic farce have taken home a Presidential Medal of Freedom. George Tenet, the CIA director who maintained that the case for invading Iraq was a "slam dunk," got his medal in 2004, as did L. Paul Bremer, the American proconsul under whose administration occupied Iraq slid into chaos. (Dick Cheney and Donald Rumsfeld had already won the medal for stints in previous administrations as Secretary of Defense.) And let us not forget Tony Blair, given the award in 2010 by Barack Obama. The list of recipients reads like a Who's Who of the past decade's foreign policy mayhem.

If there's one thing to learn from the last ten years, it's that government secrecy and lies come at a very high price in blood and money. And though information is powerless on its own, it is still a necessary precondition for any democratic state to function. Thanks to the whistleblowing revelations attributed to Bradley Manning, we have a far clearer picture of what our own country is doing. If Manning is responsible for the Wikileaks revelations, then for his gift to the republic, purchased at great price, he deserves not prison, but a Presidential Medal of Freedom, an apology from the government that has persecuted him and the heartfelt gratitude of the citizens of his country.

2

THE LIFE OF BRADLEY MANNING

(03:31:33 PM) **bradass87**: I prefer a painful truth over any blissful fantasy.

Forward Operating Base Hammer was a tough deployment. Even with the espresso bar, the workout room, high-speed internet in all the tents, the musical combos that came together and apart again when the soldiers were deployed elsewhere; even with a visit from Washington Redskin cheerleaders over Thanksgiving 2007, or any of the college squads who visited for MWR (Morale Welfare and Recreation), FOB Hammer was a tough deployment. Built in early 2007 for the "Surge" of additional US troops into an exploding Iraq, the base is forty miles east of Baghdad in the middle of the Mada'in Qada desert. There is not a hut or hamlet in sight. The isolation is no accident: the base was sited deep into nowhere to minimize the bootprint that a garrison of foreign troops would leave on Iraqi hearts and minds.

It's a desolate place. "The base was in the middle of the desert. There was sand everywhere, we had dust storms quite often, I don't know, once a month or so while I was there," said Jimmy Rodriguez to *The Guardian*. "Just a bleak place, everything was *brown* over there."[1] Rodriguez was born in the Dominican Republic and since his return to civilian life has been working at a boxing gym in New York while apprenticing as a carpenter. Rodriguez's impression of FOB Hammer is widely shared. "There was a fog that would come in almost every morning that was pollution from nearby," says Jacob Sullivan, who served as a biological and chemical weapons expert with the Second Battalion Special Brigade, redeploying home with the rank of Private First Class. Sullivan comes from Phoenix, Arizona and is now back there again, a full-time university student with entrepreneurial aspirations. "[The fog] smelled sour and nasty, and would just wave through and linger, and create an eerie atmosphere."[2]

The tedium of landscape is by all accounts a pretty good metaphor for the monotony of a deployment at FOB Hammer. "Life on base for many of the FOBbits—that's what they're called—was really very boring, with nothing to do but work, eat and sleep, and the work was twelve, fourteen hour shifts with the same people, day after day," says Peter Van Buren, a State Department Official who was posted at the base from October 2009 to May 2010. "There were a lot of *Groundhog Day* jokes." Van Buren's in northern Virginia now, having just been squeezed out of the State Department after two decades in the Foreign service, with stints in Taiwan, Japan, Korea, the UK and Hong Kong. (Van Buren's sin was linking to one of the thousands of leaked State Department documents on his personal blog, a violation of official policy; his real crime was publishing a scabrous memoir of reconstruction follies in Iraq.) During his time in Iraq he saw a lot more of the country than most of the people at Hammer. "I got outside the wire several times a week, but a lot of the FOBbits never left the base at all during their whole deployment. They got flown into Baghdad under cover of night, and a year later got flown out, also at night. For many soldiers, the base was all they ever saw of Iraq."[3] It bears repeating: a deployment at FOB Hammer was no great adventure. "Morale I think was generally really low for everyone that was there that I talked to," says Rodriguez. "All the soldiers, they didn't like it, nobody had a purpose out there."

The harsh climate doesn't help any. Temperatures can hit 100 degrees even in springtime, said another soldier, "but I'd prefer the heat over the peanut butter that forms when it rains... I grow three inches in height when it rains here." These are the observations of Pfc. Bradley E. Manning, an Army intelligence analyst who served at FOB Hammer from October 2009 till late June 2010. Manning is brainy, and he kind of knows it. ("I don't think 99% of the people I work with would make such observations.") He also has a habit of thinking for himself, which can be a liability in the military. During his deployment, which lasted from October 2009 till late June 2010, Manning spent many long shifts at a computer terminal inside the base's SCIF (pronounced "skiff," for Sensitive Compartmented Information Facility), where access is granted only to those with security clearance. Like many of his fellow FOBbits, Manning was, by his own admission, pretty miserable for much of his deployment.

Today, Bradley Manning's name is notorious, cursed and exalted. In America, elite politicians have called for his execution, and former ACLU bigwigs have eagerly admonished us "to be tough on the people in the government who are like Manning."[4] Fierce defenders have also stepped forward, among them veterans, peace activists, writers and intellectuals—a sprinkling of solidarity groups have sprouted up across the nation—across the world, in fact. The months of extreme solitary confinement inflicted on Manning made the State Department's head public relations spokesperson, normally a bland font of official euphemism, erupt in a diatribe against the punishment, which led swiftly to his resignation. Abroad, Pfc. Manning has inspired passionate defenses on the floor of the German Bundestag, earned enthusiastic plaudits from the staid Council of Europe and won a major British newspaper's readership vote for the 2011 Nobel Peace Prize—and by a wide margin.[5] Bradley Manning has been denounced as an immature, treasonous, pathological headcase who embodies why gays and lesbians should never be allowed in the military. (Manning is gay, and according to as yet unauthenticated instant-message chatlogs, he was seeking to commence male-to-female gender transition at the time of his arrest.) Manning has also been praised as a whistleblower, a patriot and a hero who sacrificed his freedom for the honor of his military, the good of his country and the world's enlightenment—a young lion of dissent against state secrecy and imperial violence.

But before he allegedly exfiltrated the Iraq War Logs (including the gruesome "Collateral Murder" helicopter gunsight video), the Afghan War logs, and 251,287 State Department cables from the SCIF at Hammer and passed them all to Wikileaks; before he become a hate-figure and a public enemy; before he became an icon, a cause and an international hero, Bradley Manning too came from somewhere.

Crescent, Oklahoma is the kind of place that lazy metropolitan journalists often respond to with Gertrude Stein's shopworn laugh-line that "there is no there there." Of course, Oklahoma is dense with historical there-ness, being both terminus of the Cherokee Nation's Trail of Tears and origin of the great Dust Bowl exodus. As journalist Denver Nicks was the first to point out, Bradley Manning isn't even the first gay whistleblower of stature to pass through this small town: before him there was Karen

Silkwood, the trade unionist who worked at the now-defunct Kerr-McGee plutonium processing plant, also in Crescent.[6] After taking note of safety failures at the plant, she died in a mysterious car crash while driving to meet a reporter from the *New York Times* on the night of November 13, 1974. This small town of 1,400 people has a rock-solid claim to be the queer whistleblower capital of the world. The red dirt of Oklahoma has bred hardy rebels, from Woody Guthrie to Ralph Ellison to Clara Luper.

Not to mention Angie Debo, the whistleblowing historian from Marshall (pop. 354) whose 1940 masterpiece, *And Still the Waters Run*, chronicles how local whites stole vast portions of the state from the Indians.[7] Her book named plenty of locally prominent names, had its initial publishing contract canceled and got the author blacklisted from teaching in Oklahoma universities. Debo, who came to Oklahoma in a covered wagon in 1899 at the age of nine and died in Marshall in 1988, has since become a revered local hero whose work is now quoted in gubernatorial inauguration speeches.

More prosaically, Crescent is a bedroom community about an hour's drive north of Oklahoma City. Although the camera crew of PBS "Frontline" made a point of shooting the town's main street right at dawn, with long and lurid shadows over empty parking spaces, Crescent is far from a ghost town.

Bradley Manning (born in 1987) grew up with his parents and big sister on a few acres three miles outside the town center. A two-story house—Brad has his own bedroom—and a "hobby farm" with a couple horses, a cow, pigs and chickens; as described by his older sister to the *Washington Post*, it sounds positively idyllic.[8] His parents, Brian Manning and Susan (née Fox) Manning, met and soon married in her native Wales where Brian Manning was deployed at the Cawdor Barracks with the US Navy in the 1970s. What precisely he was doing in the military he's not allowed to say, but he had a security clearance and learned enough about computers to later land work as an IT manager with the Hertz rental car agency in Oklahoma City, a job that made him good money and took him around the world.

Young Bradley took after his father, a tech whiz from an early age, always playing with his father's hand-me-down computers. In fact he was a bit of a prodigy, reading (by his own recollection) at age three, doing multiplication and division by age four. According to family members, Manning was doing C++ programming by age eight and had designed his first website at the age of ten. Bradley took the grand prize three years running at the Crescent science fair, beating out students several grades ahead. With a few other classmates, he represented the town at "academic bowl" competitions all over the state. While other boys might be content to play video games, young Bradley liked to hack them and tweak the coding.

Bradley Manning definitely has a mind of his own. Despite being raised Catholic, the boy refused to utter the "under God" part of the Pledge of Allegiance, a startling act of freethinking for an elementary school student anywhere in the United States, let alone a small town that is heavily Evangelical. As Rick McCombs, currently the principal in Crescent, told reporter Denver Nicks, "You would say something, and he would have an opinion which was a little unusual for a middle school kid. This young man actually kind of thought on his own."[9] Sometimes he took it upon himself to correct teachers. "Well Bradley, little munchkin that he is, he would stand up for what he believes," remembers Mary Egleston, a family friend and former substitute teacher in Crescent.[10] Bradley was precociously high-minded, arguing even in elementary school that the US had a right to assert its military power overseas to protect its interests, according to hometown friend Jordan Davis. As Davis told the *Washington Post*, even the video game "Call to Power II" soon led young Manning to a serious conversation about the powers of technology to achieve democracy. "He was basically really into America," Davis told one reporter; "He wanted to serve his country." When Al Qaeda attacked New York and Washington on September 11th, 2001, Bradley Manning's friends turned to him as a source of wisdom and judgment. An independent mind joined to a deep sense of patriotic obligation is a constant in Bradley Manning's life, even as his concept of what it meant to serve his country matured with age and experience.

Bradley Manning was a child who enjoyed knowing things; he read the encyclopedia for fun. Manning learned to be a quiet child—not anti-social, but quiet. It probably didn't make Bradley's life at school any easier that he, like his father, was on the small side and grew to be 5'2". The boy got his share of bullying and abuse. And there was something else. As he later confided to a stranger over instant messaging in 2010:

(11:33:46 AM) bradass87: i didnt like getting beat up or called gay [didn't really know what gay meant, but knew it was something bad]
(11:34:06 AM) bradass87: so i joined sports teams, and started becoming an athlete

At age 13, Bradley Manning told his two closest friends that he was gay, a difficult conversation for any teenager virtually anywhere in the United States. Still, these are no different from the troubles that other young people face and overcome, hopefully with the help of a supportive family.

It is not clear that Manning ever got such support from his family. Today, his parents are in the supremely unenviable position of having their childrearing dug up and held up to the light by a curious public. How many mothers and fathers could survive this without looking

17

at least a little like monsters? And yet this is essential to the story of Bradley Manning. The locals of Crescent have had unkind things to tell reporters about Brian Manning—that he was demeaning, "a dick", verbally and physically abusive, that his son was "more afraid of his father than normal." Manning's mother was an alcoholic through much of Bradley's childhood; she told the *Washington Post* that she started the morning with vodka in her tea and finished the day with rum in her Coke. Despite living miles from town, she never learned to drive a car, and leaned heavily on her young son to write out checks to pay bills. (Her ex-husband describes her today as semi-literate.)[11] Neither parent attended parent-teacher conferences at Bradley's school, and when their son was the first Crescent student to win a statewide academic trophy in Oklahoma City, his parents were absent from the audience. And then they divorced. How they arrived at this domestic cataclysm is best told by Bradley himself from these (as yet unauthenticated) instant messages from mid-2010.

(11:34:19 AM) **bradass87:** around this time (middle school)… my parents divorced

(11:36:34 AM) **bradass87:** my father in a drunken stupor got angry with me because i was doing some noisy homework while he was watching TV… he went into his bedroom, pulled out a shotgun, and chased me out of the house… the door was deadbolted, so i couldn't get out before he caught up with me… so my mother (also wasted) threw a lamp over his head… and i proceeded to fight him, breaking his nose, and made it out of the house… my father let off one or two shots, causing damage, but injuring nobody, except for the belt lashing i got for "making him shoot up the house"

(11:36:59 AM) **bradass87:** i went to school the next day, and my teachers noticed the wounds, and got social workers involved

(11:37:11 AM) bradass87: he immediately stopped drinking, and my mother filed for divorce

(11:37:29 AM) bradass87: after the divorce, my mother attempted suicide...

(11:38:23 AM) bradass87: after taking care of her for awhile, and gaining custody of me, my mother took me to her hometown, haverfordwest, wales... to live and go to school

In Wales, Bradley found himself more an outsider than ever: still small, still nerdy, but now a foreigner with a funny accent and all the more easily bullied and ostracized. (His mother remembers Bradley going on a group camping trip only to awake in the morning to find that all the other campers had pulled up stakes and ditched him overnight.) But the outspoken independence of mind had not changed. "He always had this sense that 'I'm going to right a big wrong,'" says Welsh school friend Tom Dyer. "He was like that at school. If something went wrong, he would speak up about it if he didn't agree with something. He would even have altercations with teachers if he thought something was not right." [12] By sixteen, he achieved the British equivalent of a high-school diploma. With a few of his mates—Manning had a small circle of friends, all into computers—he tried his hand at an internet startup venture. Like the great majority of such endeavors, it went nowhere. He cared for his mother, who, ailing from a series of strokes, leaned on her son more heavily than ever. Manning was not happy. Lonely and despondent, the seventeen-year-old surprised his father in the summer of 2005 by calling him up and asking if he might have room for his son at his new home, with his new family—Brian Manning had remarried—back in Oklahoma.

Brian Manning found a job for his computer whiz son at Zoto, a software company in Tulsa. His boss, Zoto cofounder Kord Campbell, told the *Post* that he was wowed by young Manning's skills, and by his adult intellect. With the Iraq War becoming more unpopular by the day, international politics were a topic of conversation everywhere in America, and Bradley had a point of view. "Here I was, a grown man, and he could run circles around me" talking about Iraq and Afghanistan, Campbell told the *Post*. "He didn't like that people were being killed, particularly the citizens, innocent people. I remember us specifically talking about how we were having a hard time getting information on how many people were being killed." Campbell seems to have gone above and beyond to help his young employee along, even taking time to teach Bradley how to drive. But though Bradley had the computer skills, the teenager did not have the emotional stability to hold down an adult nine-to-five job. Campbell recalls Bradley zoning out and going catatonic on the job, and with reluctance, he had to let the boy go. (Manning's version is a little different; he later told a friend that "it was company funding and lack of manpower that killed my job at zoto… Flickr creamed us because my boss was a marketing retard;" he also claimed to have proposed an engine that would convert uploaded videos and stream them through Flash, i.e. YouTube before it was a reality, but that his boss didn't heed his young intern's advice.)

At home, tensions grew, and he fought with his father and stepmother about money, his smoking, his attitude, his sexuality. After one particularly energetic row, she called the police. The next day, Manning left, later telling a reporter at a rally against Don't Ask Don't Tell in Syracuse, New York that he was thrown out of the house for being gay;[13] his father denied that his son's sexual orientation had anything to do with it.[14] An unemployed adult child made to leave home after friction with a stepparent: it's a scene that plays out every day in every state of the union.

Bradley fled to Tulsa, moved in briefly with his boyhood pal Jordan Davis and took minimum-wage service jobs. He drifted to Chicago, doing odd jobs there. He was a pícaro, a Joad without the family, a homeless kid on his own who slept in his pickup in the O'Hare parking lot. He was all alone. There are thousands in America like him.

In the spring of 2006, Bradley moved in with his father's sister in the Washington DC area. He got a job in retail at an Abercrombie & Fitch shop, and then a better job behind the counter at Starbucks. He enrolled in a local community college, then dropped out after doing poorly on an exam. "He was extremely organized, extremely tidy," his aunt told the *Washington Post*. "This was not somebody who was flailing around." He networked with people in the DC political world—staffers, people on the hill. He liked to know things; he liked to know what was going on politically.

Then, in late 2007, Bradley Manning did the last thing that anyone would expect of a 5´2´´ openly gay nineteen-year-old with a fierce independent streak.

He enlisted.

Why do so, and in addition do so in the middle of a shooting war that to all indications he did not approve of? We have already noted Bradley Manning's high-minded spirit of service to his country, a spirit far removed from chauvinistic nationalism that often passes for patriotism in America today. Then there is the example of his father, however estranged, still exerting a strong gravitational pull on the teenage son. (Brian Manning admitted to a PBS "Frontline" correspondent that he did twist his son's arm a bit to get him to enlist and give his life some direction.[15])

Like all the other soldiers he wound up with at FOB Hammer, Brad Manning wanted to get something out of the army aside from the fulfillment of patriotic duty. Peter Van Buren, the foreign service officer who overlapped with Manning at Hammer, recalled the soldiers there: "Each of them was proud to serve but each of them had at least another reason that they carried around for joining the military, their own little secret weight.[...] Ran away from an evil girlfriend, needed money for college, father said get a job or get out, that sort of thing."[16] Bradley Manning could check more than one of these boxes.

Bradley wanted to go to college, but he had no money and apparently no financial support from home. With the GI Bill, the Army could pay his tuition later. (When deployed at Fort Drum in upstate New York, he told a friend "i hope i can SOMEHOW get into a nice university and study physics for a bachelors or masters (doctorate if im smart enough?)" He dreamt of "those fancy sounding colleges [...] UC Berkely, Carnegie Mellon, MIT, University Chicago." He even exhorted his friend to think seriously about going to college; after all, "someone like me is spending 4 years in the military just to get the opportunity."

Manning reported for basic training at Fort Leonard Wood in Missouri in October, 2007. How would he fare in the army, this 5'2" eighteen-year-old with an independent mind and mouth, a young man whose sexual orientation was not so difficult to detect?

In basic training, Bradley Manning stood out. The drill sergeants picked on him. He fought back; it's his way. They picked on him some more. Before long, Manning found himself in the "discharge unit"—the separate barracks for soldiers who have essentially flunked basic training and are being "outprocessed," that is, rejected and expelled from the military.

A team of investigative reporters at *The Guardian* newspaper found a contemporary of Manning's from the Fort Leonard Wood discharge unit. It is worth quoting at length from *The Guardian's* interview with the discharged soldier who knew Bradley Manning.

The kid was barely 5 feet—he was a runt. And by military standards and compared with everyone who was around there—he was a runt. By military standards, "he's a runt, so pick on him," or "he's crazy—pick on him," or "he's a faggot—pick on him." The guy took it from every side. He couldn't please anyone. And he tried. He really did. [...]

He wasn't a soldier—there wasn't anything about him that was a soldier. He has this idea that he was going in and that he was going to be pushing papers and he was gonna be some super smart computer guy and that he was gonna be important, that he was gonna matter to someone and he was gonna matter to something. And he got there and realized that he didn't matter and that none of that was going to happen. [...]

He was in the DU. That means he was not bouncing back. He was going home. You don't just accidentally end up in a Discharge Unit one day. You have somebody saying, "You know what, he is no good—let's get him out of here. There are a lot of steps to go to before you even hit a DU let alone before you go from a DU to a bus or a plane home. [...]

The DU at any given time had about 100+ men. It was basically one big room, it had a group of bunks, bunk-beds and that's where we all lived.

He was being picked on—that was one part of it. Because you know Bradley—everybody said he was crazy or he was faking and the biggest part of it all was when rumors were getting around that he was chapter 15—you know, homosexual. They'd call him a faggot or call him a chapter 15—in the military world, being called a chapter 15 is like a civilian being called a faggot to their face in the street. [...]

For Bradley, it was rough. To say it was rough is an understatement. He was targeted [...] by bullies, by the drill sergeants. Basically he was targeted by anybody who was within arm's reach of him.

There was a small percentage, I'd say maybe 10–15 guys tops, who didn't care what chapter he was, who just wanted to coexist until they could get out and just get along. But the rest of them—we're talking mentally unfit. Some of them were there for criminal charges. Everyone who was there was getting kicked out. And between being mentally unfit and mentally unstable and being criminal, and then being locked in this room with the guys saying, "Oh, here's this little guy"—it was open season on him. Being gay—being Bradley Manning and being gay in the DU—it was hostile. He was constantly on edge, constantly on guard. [...]

They have all these beds and bunks that are all lined up and at the front there's a common area. It's not much of a common area but there's a desk and doors, bathroom, storage room and then the entrance to this place. And there were three guys who had him cornered up front, and they were picking on him and he was yelling and screaming back.

And we got there—it was me and a couple of other guys who went up there to start breaking it up—and I'm yelling, "Get the hell out of here, back off." And I started pulling Manning off him while the other guys were taking care of the ones who were picking on him. And I got Manning off to the side and yeah, he pissed himself. That wasn't the only time he did that, but that was the time I remember. It happened a few other times, I know a couple of guys who could tell you the same story.[17]

Manning seems plainly not to have been soldier material. But he was not discharged. Instead, he was "recycled" back into the system. The unnamed soldier from the Fort Leonard Wood discharge unit had thoughts about this, too:

There is something wrong with the system. First off, I was in the DU for a month and in that entire month no one person was recycled from the DU. When I got out, I went home and I was getting periodic phone calls from the guys. Bradley was the only one who got recycled. And like I said, for the life of me I still don't understand how or why. [...] I think I am saying what is wrong with the system. Why was the US Army in such a mess that they were recycling the likes of Bradley Manning?

I know for a fact that in 2007 recruiting numbers were the lowest they had ever been. They were lowering recruitment standards like crazy. I mean, facial tattoos, too tall, too short, too fat, criminal record—it didn't matter. [...] It was take everybody you could get. Keep hold of everybody you can get.

I can't help Bradley out. I tried to help him out then. A few others of us did but I can't do anything to help him. [...] I'm just saying a lot of people let him down. He is not the first one they let down and he is not the last one. That shit is going on right now at Fort Leonard Wood, Missouri. It is going on at Fort Sill, Oklahoma and it is going on everywhere there is a training facility.[18]

At the end of his trials at Fort Leonard Wood, Bradley Manning moved one step closer to the SCIF at FOB Hammer.

With desperate optimism, Manning told a friend (according to the *Washington Post*) that he was sure that intelligence training in Fort Huachuca would be better. "I'm going to be with people more like me." And he did enjoy intelligence training. He was mildly reprimanded for broadcasting information about the base that might be considered sensitive on YouTube. But he still got a top-secret security clearance, and in August 2008 joined the 2nd Brigade, 10th Mountain Division at Fort Drum in far-upstate New York. Another step closer to the SCIF.

At Fort Drum, Private Manning was a paradox the military was scarcely able to digest. On the one hand, he was wholly committed to his work as a soldier. He was doing "computations and analytical work," he told a friend, and preparing weekly intelligence briefings for the commander. He saw his role in the military as a protector of human life, and it was a mission he believed in: "I feel a great responsibility and duty to people. [...] I'm more concerned about making sure that everyone, soldiers, marines, contractor [sic], even the local nationals, get home to their families." It was more than a task; it was a calling, a life. He fervently believed in the power of intellectual development to help him carry out his duties to his fellow soldier, to his fellow human.

> im reading a lot more, delving deeper into philosophy, art, physics, biology, politics then i ever did in school... whats even better with my current position is that i can apply what i learn to provide more information to my officers and commanders, and hopefully save lives... i figure that justifies my sudden choice to this[.][19]

What we know about Manning's time at Fort Drum comes largely from a series of instant-message chats he held over several months with a Chicago youth named Zach Antolak who posts her thoughts in drag as Zinnia Jones on YouTube. Manning reached out to and told her—she is a sympathetic listener—about himself. Revealing conversations with a total stranger who becomes a virtual friend; it is a practice common among Bradley's generation, and it later brought him to grief.

Manning spent his weekend leave in Boston; he found a steady Brandeis undergraduate boyfriend and a social niche among the idealistic wing of the IT crowd, young people who believed in the emancipatory potential of digital technology and communications. Manning demonstrated against the Don't Ask Don't Tell policy designed to keep gays closeted in the military. He found a world of hip young people, where being gay and brainy is perfectly natural, perfectly normal.

But away from the libertarian paradise of Boston's undergraduate scene, Bradley Manning did not fit in with quotidian military life at Fort

Drum. He couldn't get along with roommates, one of whom he thought was homophobic, another racist. He was written up for tossing chairs around in a fit of rage. He was written up for yelling at his superiors. He was required to get mental health counseling. Was Manning aware of the clash between his ideal of patriotic service and the reality of actual military life? Sometimes he was:

> i actually believe what the army tries to make itself out to be: a diverse place full of people defending the country... male, female, black, white, gay, straight, christian, jewish, asian, old or young, it doesn't matter to me; we all wear the same green uniform... but its still a male-dominated, christian-right, oppressive institution, with a few hidden jems [sic] of diversity.

Eventually Manning's vision of the American military as a global protector of freedom came under strain. As one of his Boston friends told the *Washington Post*, Manning "expressed a feeling to me like how messed up the situation is [in Iraq]. He said things like, 'If more people knew what was going on over there, they would not support the war.'"

According to his superiors at Fort Drum, Manning was not working out as a soldier, and they discussed keeping him back when his unit was deployed to Iraq. However, in the fall of 2009, the occupation was desperate for intelligence analysts with computer skills, and Private Bradley Manning, his superiors hurriedly concluded, showed signs of improvement as a workable soldier. This is how, on October 10, 2009, Private First Class Bradley Manning was deployed to FOB Hammer in Iraq as an intelligence analyst.

Upon arrival at FOB Hammer, Bradley Manning was happy: finally, he saw a chance to use his training and skills to keep people out of harm's way in the middle of a shooting war. In the SCIF where Manning did his tasks, a large windowless warehouse full of computers and desks and power cords, there were moments of intense and earnest teamwork. Much of the time, though, the SCIF is a big room full of bored soldiers working twelve to fourteen hour shifts, day after day.

There was entertainment available in the system. According to former FOBbit Jimmy Rodriguez, "This stuff was all in a folder. It had a generic name on it so no one would look into it. A mix of games, sex and violence. They loved to watch these clips of Apaches gunning down people and whatnot. It was definitely entertainment."[20] The whole base environment was heavily mediatised, with a live-feed projection from a drone flying over Iraq up on a big screen in the Op Center. "It was mesmeric," says Van Buren. "We called it 'war porn,' though I never saw actual shooting on screen."

At first Manning thrived in his new setting. He privately informed his supervisor that he was gay, according to a Boston friend, and the supervisor told him it didn't matter as long as the soldier did his job well. Though still freely posting LGBT-supportive messages on his Facebook page, Manning was discreet about his sexual orientation on base. It really wasn't clear that anyone cared. "From my time on the base, I'm not sure how important that gay or straight was to any of the soldiers," says Van Buren. "What people are really worried about is whether their fellow soldier is reliable, and can do their job."[21]

Manning had access to SIPRNet, the Secret Internet Protocol Router Network, used by the Defense Department and the State Department to transfer classified data, and to JWICS, the Joint Worldwide Intelligence Communications System. In November he was promoted to the rank of specialist, when he began to learn the true meaning of success in his line of work.

We know this because by November, Manning had made internet contact with an American "gender counselor": the soldier was considering gender transition. As momentous and potentially wrenching as this decision can be, it was not what troubled Manning. As the therapist told *New York Magazine*, what was upsetting the young intel analyst was his work: specifically, a targeting mission in Basra that turned ugly. "Two groups of locals were converging in this one area. Manning was trying to figure out why they were meeting," said the counselor to *New York* journalist Steve Fishman. From the SCIF, Manning advised an Army unit to move in quickly; it did. "Ultimately, some guy loosely connected to the group got killed," said the counselor, and Manning felt deeply complicit in the bloodshed.

Manning's real Damascene moment came when he investigated the arrest of Iraqi civilian protesters for an act of faultless good citizenship. He later confided the whole story to someone he believed to be a friend:

(02:31:02 PM) bradass87: i think the thing that got me the most... that made me rethink the world more than anything

(02:35:46 PM) bradass87: was watching 15 detainees taken by the Iraqi Federal Police... for printing "anti-Iraqi literature"... the iraqi federal police wouldn't cooperate with US forces, so i was instructed to investigate the matter, find out who the "bad guys" were, and how significant this was for the FPs... it turned out, they had printed a scholarly critique against PM Maliki... i had an interpreter read it for me... and when i found out that it was a benign political critique titled "Where did the money go?" and following the corruption trail within the PM's cabinet... i immediately took that information and *ran* to the officer to explain what was going on... he didn't want to hear any of it... he told me to shut up and explain how we could assist the FPs in finding *MORE* detainees...

(02:36:27 PM) bradass87: everything started slipping after that... i saw things differently

(02:37:37 PM) bradass87: i had always questioned the things worked, and investigated to find the truth... but that was a point where i was a *part* of something... i was actively involved in something that i was completely against...

The arrest of nonviolent civilians was of particular concern because torture, as Manning well knew, remained a common practice among the Iraqi authorities even six years into the American occupation. (The gruesome facts of Iraqi torture were amply documented by the US military in documents that were later released by Wikileaks.) True, then-Chairman of the Joint Chiefs General Peter Pace had in December 2005 publicly contradicted Secretary of Defense Donald Rumsfeld by declaring that it was the duty of every US soldier in Iraq to stop torture if he or she saw it happening. (Pace's tenure as Chairman of the Joint Chiefs was not renewed for a second term.) But when it came to actually enforcing this rule, the whole chain of command in Iraq turned out to be remarkably easygoing. Pace's mandate was hollowed out anyway by Rumsfeld's own secret legal directives in the form of Fragmentary Order 242, which set forth a specific policy of non-interference in Iraqi torture. Deployment to the war zone taught Manning that military occupation is, by its very nature, less protective than predatory.

Gunsight videos of Iraqis getting blown away by AH-64 Apache gunships were ambient "entertainment" inside the SCIF. Like so many others, Manning watched one such video shot from over half a mile above the outskirts of Baghdad on July 12, 2007. In the video, a group of civilians mingling with insurgents is fired upon by a gunship. Wounded Iraqis crawling away are shot dead. A van comes by to retrieve the wounded, and the helicopter opens fire on it too. The van turns out to be full of children. Throughout the gunsight video, pilot and crew are cracking wise, nervously, gleefully, callously. "Look at all those dead guys." "Well, it's their fault for bringing their kids into a battle." When the thirty-nine minute video is over, at least eleven people have been killed, most of them unarmed civilians. Two of the civilians killed turn out to be Reuters News Agency employees; the company files a FOIA request to find out about the death but is stonewalled. *Washington Post* reporter David Finkel gets a copy of the video and writes about it in his book *The Good Soldiers*—which Manning will read—but Finkel is unable or unwilling to release the video. This is just one incident in a war that has, by conservative estimates, killed over 100,000 Iraqi civilians. Bradley Manning did not see this video as entertainment. He dug deeper.

(03:10:32 PM) bradass87: at first glance... it was just a bunch of guys getting shot up by a helicopter... no big deal... about two dozen more where that came from right... but something struck me as odd with the van thing... and also the fact it was being stored in a JAG officer's directory... so i looked into it... eventually tracked down the date, and then the exact GPS co-ord... and i was like... ok, so thats what happened... cool... then i went to the regular internet... and it was still on my mind... so i typed into goog... the date, and the location... and then i see this http://www.nytimes.com/2007/07/13/world/middleeast/13iraq.html

Manning's dreams of using his skills to safeguard human life died hard. He decided to do something about it.

(03:07:01 PM) bradass87: i just... couldnt let these things stay inside of the system... and inside of my head...
(03:07:26 PM) bradass87: i recognized the value of some things...
(03:11:07 PM) bradass87: i kept that in my mind for weeks... probably a month and a half... before i forwarded it to them

The "them" was Wikileaks.

It is not clear when Bradley Manning allegedly began transmitting documents to Wikileaks; the government in its charge sheet against the private claims it was November 2009. By then, the anti-secrecy group had already achieved celebrity in tech-libertarian and media circles by publishing the Yahoo email account of Sarah Palin and various 9–11 text messages sent from inside the burning towers. Founded in 2006, the website offers a place for whistleblowers around the world to post important revelations, with source anonymity protected by the latest encryption technology. The site's content is backed up by mirror-sites around the world. Wikileaks is by no means the first such site; before it came Cryptome—and it will surely not be the last.

On April 5, 2010, Wikileaks premiered the helicopter video at the National Press Club in Washington DC, slapping the gratuitous title "Collateral Murder" on the clip. In days, millions of people around the world watched the video, and for the most part responded in horror and disgust. America's international lawyers rushed to provide the disquieting assurance that the aerial assault was in perfect conformity with the laws of armed conflict. A few members of the helicopter crew stepped forward to apologize to the families of the Iraqi dead and wounded. America still had 98,000 troops in Iraq (not counting mercenaries and other contractors), and their purpose there was questioned anew. Bradley Manning saw all of this. He became Facebook friends with the American infantryman, Ethan McCord, who at the scene of the aerial attack went back to the shot-up van to retrieve two wounded children and rushed them to a hospital. Manning felt a loop had been closed:

(02:07:41 AM) bradass87: event occurs in 2007, i watch video in 2009 with no context, do research, forward information to group of FOI activists, more research occurs, video is released in 2010, those involved come forward to discuss event, i witness those involved coming forward to discuss publicly, even add them as friends on FB... without them knowing who i am

(02:08:37 AM) bradass87: they touch my life, i touch their life, they touch my life again... full circle

The "Collateral Murder" video is only the beginning of what Manning allegedly exfiltrated to Wikileaks. There are the Afghan War Logs, 91,731 "Significant Action" military field reports that provide a mosaic for a pacification campaign going poorly. There are the Iraq War Logs, 391,832 more SigAct field reports, another pointillist portrait of a failed campaign. And 251, 287 State Department cables, most of which are not classified, many of which are "confidential" and some six percent of which are "secret." (Not one of the documents that Bradley Manning has allegedly disclosed is "top secret.")

How might he have done it? In fact, sending hundreds of thousands of documents from the SCIF at FOB Hammer would have been easy. The "infosec"—information security—at FOB Hammer was not so much faulty as nonexistent. As former FOBbit Jacob Sullivan remembered:

> There were laptops sitting there with passwords on sticky notes. If someone in uniform came in and sits beside me at a computer and I didn't know him, I'm not going to stop him and say excuse me, can I see some ID, I'm just gonna be like, "whatever."[22]

And Manning himself in these unauthenticated chatlogs is even more candid about the wholesale absence of security at the SCIF.

(02:00:12 PM) bradass87: everyone just sat at their workstations... watching music videos / car chases / buildings exploding... and writing more stuff to CD/DVD... the culture fed opportunities

(02:01:44 PM) bradass87: hardest part is arguably internet access... uploading any sensitive data over the open internet is a bad idea... since networks are monitored for any insurgent/terrorist/militia/criminal types (01:52:30 PM) bradass87: funny thing is... we transffered [sic] so much data on unmarked CDs...

(01:52:42 PM) bradass87: everyone did... videos... movies... music (01:53:05 PM) bradass87: all out in the open

(01:53:53 PM) bradass87: bringing CDs too [sic] and from the networks was/is a common phenomeon

(01:54:14 PM) info@adrianlamo.com: is that how you got the cables out?

(01:54:28 PM) bradass87: perhaps

(01:54:42 PM) bradass87: i would come in with music on a CD-RW

(01:55:21 PM) bradass87: labelled with something like "Lady Gaga"... erase the music... then write a compressed split file

(01:55:46 PM) bradass87: no-one suspected a thing

(01:55:48 PM) bradass87: =L kind of sad

(01:56:04 PM) info@adrianlamo.com: and odds are, they never will

(01:56:07 PM) bradass87: i didnt even have to hide anything

(01:56:36 PM) info@adrianlamo.com: from a professional perspective, i'm curious how the server they were on was insecure

(01:57:19 PM) bradass87: you had people working 14 hours a day... every single day... no weekends... no recreation...

(01:57:27 PM) bradass87: people stopped caring after 3 weeks

Career foreign service member Peter Van Buren condemned the lack of security to me. "It's lax that no one ever disabled the disk drives in the SCIF computers, and the idea that anyone could *burn* a disc in there is insane, and breaks every single security rule."[23]

This amazing lack of "infosec" has been a major point among pundits and journalists horrified that the leaks' information was brought to light.

For those who welcome the disclosures, what is more disturbing still is how it took so long for these documents to be leaked. After all, some three million Americans have a security clearance: did none of these people who came into contact with the "Collateral Murder" video see fit to release it to the public? Until Manning's alleged leaks, there apparently was no need for infosec measures, given how thoroughly those with a security clearance had internalized the government's mindset.

Back at base, Bradley Manning's career as a soldier—his only ticket to the university education he craved—was fast disintegrating. By May 5, his superiors thought he was behaving erratically; they removed the bolt from his service rifle. He was more and more intent on gender transition, which he could only commence outside the military. On May 7, Manning slugged a female superior in the face: he was demoted back to Private First Class, sent to work in the supply room—but retained his security clearance. He was soon to be discharged, for adjustment disorder ("in lieu of 'gender identity disorder'," he'd later say), and he was very, very lonely.

Pfc. Bradley Manning reached out to a stranger.

On May 21, Bradley Manning contacted Adrian Lamo, a renowned computer hacker whose name was accidentally released in a Wikileaks fundraising missive. Surely Lamo, a famous hacker, once convicted on felony charges for his digital mischief, would understand the greatness of Manning's alleged achievement. Besides, Lamo was bi; he has an ex who is male-to-female transgender; he has another ex who was counterintelligence in the army. Manning and Lamo flirted a little. Manning related his life story, his aspirations, his reasons for disclosing the documents. They joked about Lamo turning Manning in to the authorities.

What Manning didn't know was that two days into the conversation, Lamo in fact went to the federal authorities. And his handlers were obviously feeding him questions to ask Manning—"in all seriousness, would you shoot if MP's showed up?" On May 29, military police came to FOB Hammer to arrest Bradley Manning, who was soon taken to Kuwait for further interrogation under detention.

For turning in Bradley Manning, Adrian Lamo has been cast both as a responsible, patriotic citizen and a duplicitous snitch. (He introduced himself to Manning as a journalist and a minister, free to take confessions in confidentiality. Was this a joke, or sarcasm? Did Manning ever believe it?) Famous as Lamo is inside hacking circles, to those outside that sphere he simply resembles other police informants: a convicted felon with a history of mental illness. (Lamo was involuntarily committed in California just a few weeks before his chats with Manning.[24]) Lamo has defended his decision to turn in Manning with a mix of faux-worldly cynicism and high-minded patriotism, neither quite ringing true. Adrian Lamo had much to lose from being implicated in another felony, especially the greatest security breach in United States history. He most likely turned in his new and unsolicited acquaintance to protect himself from a prison sentence. How many of us, in Lamo's situation, would do otherwise?

The lengthy chatlogs between Lamo and Manning are the primary document of Manning's life, his alleged leaks and motives. But for the amazing deeds they recount, the chatlogs read like the typical diary of an intelligent, intense, earnest twenty-two-year-old. The intel analyst's intent is conscious, coherent, historically informed and above all it is *political*. These segments of the chatlogs are worth quoting at length, as they have for the most part been studiously ignored by a mass media determined not to comprehend Bradley Manning's motives.

(12:15:11 PM) bradass87: hypothetical question: if you had free reign over classified networks for long periods of time... say, 8–9 months... and you saw incredible things, awful things... things that belonged in the public domain, and not on some server stored in a dark room in Washington DC... what would you do?

(12:16:38 PM) bradass87: or Guantanamo, Bagram, Bucca, Taji, VBC for that matter...

(12:17:47 PM) bradass87: things that would have an impact on 6.7 billion people

(12:21:24 PM) bradass87: say... a database of half a million events during the iraq war... from 2004 to 2009... with reports, date time groups, lat-lon locations, casualty figures... ? or 260,000 state department cables from embassies and consulates all over the world, explaining how the first world exploits the third, in detail, from an internal perspective?

[...]

(12:52:33 PM) bradass87: Hilary Clinton, and several thousand diplomats around the world are going to have a heart attack when they wake up one morning, and finds an entire repository of classified foreign policy is available, in searchable format to the public... =L

(12:53:41 PM) bradass87: s/Hilary/Hillary

(12:54:47 PM) info@adrianlamo.com: What sort of content?

[...]

(12:59:41 PM) bradass87: uhm... crazy, almost criminal political backdealings... the non-PR-versions of world events and crises... uhm... all kinds of stuff like everything from the buildup to the Iraq War during Powell, to what the actual content of "aid packages" is: for instance, PR that the US is sending aid to pakistan includes funding for water/food/clothing... that much is true, it includes that, but the other 85% of it is for F-16 fighters and munitions to aid in the Afghanistan effort, so the US can call in Pakistanis to do aerial bombing instead of americans potentially killing civilians and creating a PR crisis

(1:00:57 PM) bradass87: theres so much... it affects everybody on earth... everywhere there's a US post... there's a diplomatic scandal that will be revealed... Iceland, the Vatican, Spain, Brazil, Madagascar, if its a country, and its recognized by the US as a country, its got dirt on it

[...]

(1:10:38 PM) bradass87: its open diplomacy... world-wide anarchy in CSV format... its Climategate with a global scope, and breathtaking depth... its beautiful, and horrifying...

(1:11:54 PM) bradass87: and... its important that it gets out... i feel, for some bizarre reason

(1:12:02 PM) bradass87: it might actually change something

[...]

(03:15:38 PM) bradass87: i dont know... im just, weird i guess

(03:15:49 PM) bradass87: i cant separate myself from others

(03:16:12 PM) bradass87: i feel connected to everybody... like they were distant family

(03:16:24 PM) bradass87: i... care?

(03:17:27 PM) bradass87: http://www.kxol.com.au/images/pale_blue_dot. jpg <– sums it up for me

(03:18:17 PM) bradass87: i probably shouldn't have read sagan, feynman, and so many intellectual authors last summer...

(03:24:10 PM) bradass87: we're human... and we're killing ourselves... and no-one seems to see that... and it bothers me

(03:24:26 PM) bradass87: apathy

(03:25:28 PM) bradass87: apathy is far worse than the active participation

(03:26:23 PM) bradass87: >hug<

(03:29:31 PM) bradass87: http://vimeo.com/5081720 Elie Wiesel summed it up pretty well for me... though his story is much much more important that mine

(03:29:48 PM) bradass87: *than

(03:31:33 PM) bradass87: I prefer a painful truth over any blissful fantasy.

[...]

(03:35:44 PM) bradass87: i think ive been traumatized too much by reality, to care about consequences of shattering the fantasy

**

[..]

(02:20:57 AM) bradass87: well, it was forwarded to WL

(02:21:18 AM) bradass87: and god knows what happens now

(02:22:27 AM) bradass87: hopefully worldwide discussion, debates, and reforms

(02:23:06 AM) bradass87: if not... than we're doomed

(02:23:18 AM) bradass87: as a species

(02:24:13 AM) bradass87: i will officially give up on the society we have if nothing happens

(02:24:58 AM) bradass87: the reaction to the video gave me immense hope... CNN's iReport was overwhelmed... Twitter exploded...

(02:25:18 AM) bradass87: people who saw, knew there was something wrong

[...]

(02:28:10 AM) bradass87: i want people to see the truth... regardless of who they are... because without information, you cannot make informed decisions as a public

**

(02:23:25 PM) bradass87: i could've sold to russia or china, and made bank?

(02:23:36 PM) info@adrianlamo.com: why didn't you?

(02:23:58 PM) bradass87: because it's public data

(02:24:15 PM) info@adrianlamo.com: i mean, the cables

(02:24:46 PM) bradass87: it belongs in the public domain

(02:25:15 PM) bradass87: information should be free

(02:25:39 PM) bradass87: it belongs in the public domain

(02:26:18 PM) bradass87: because another state would just take advantage of the information... try and get some edge

(02:26:55 PM) bradass87: if its out in the open... it should be a public good

(02:27:04 PM) bradass87: *do the

(02:27:23 PM) bradass87: rather than some slimy intel collector

(02:29:18 PM) bradass87: im crazy like that

**

(04:42:16 PM) bradass87: im not sure whether i'd be considered a type of "hacker", "cracker", "hacktivist", "leaker" or what...

(04:42:26 PM) bradass87: im just me... really

(05:52:52 PM) info@adrianlamo.com: You're a leftist, I take it. Not a bad thing. My dad has a book signed by Philip Agee.

(05:53:09 PM) bradass87: i dont have a doctrine

(05:53:40 PM) bradass87: socialism / capitalism are the same thing in practice

(05:53:57 PM) info@adrianlamo.com: Everyone does. Our beliefs place us somewhere, even if it's "centrist"

(05:54:15 PM) bradass87: i know i do, but i havent quite defined it

(05:54:17 PM) info@adrianlamo.com: except apathetic

(05:54:42 PM) bradass87: apathy is its own 3rd dimension... i have special graph for that... =P

(05:54:56 PM) info@adrianlamo.com: I'm a fan of of realpolitik myself.

(05:55:10 PM) bradass87: i dont quite know

(05:55:34 PM) bradass87: seen too much reality to be "polar"

(05:56:02 PM) **bradass87:** i dont like dogma, thats one thing i can say without doubt…

After two months' interrogation at Camp Arifjan in Kuwait, Bradley Manning was transferred stateside to the prison at Marine Corps Base at Quantico, Virginia. The disclosures were a sensation—less perhaps for their content than for the story surrounding them—Wikileaks, Assange, Manning himself. Manning was famous.

Days before Manning's transfer to Quantico, Wikileaks released the Afghan War logs in partnership with *The Guardian, Der Spiegel* and the *New York Times*, posting 75,000 of the 91,731 documents on their website. (The rest were withheld to minimize risk to individuals named in the reports.) Wikileaks and Julian Assange instantly became hate-figures for most of the American media and political elite. Even liberals like David Letterman and Rachel Maddow proclaimed their dislike of Assange. On the neoconservative right, the reaction was vociferous: Newt Gingrich said Assange "should be treated as an enemy combatant and Wikileaks should be closed down permanently and decisively"; *Weekly Standard* editor Bill Kristol asked "Why can't we use our various assets to harass, snatch or neutralize Julian Assange and his collaborators, wherever they are?" Reactions among Democrats were not much milder. Democratic political consultant Bob Beckel opined that there was only one way to deal with Assange: "illegally shoot the son of a bitch." In the same twenty-four hour period, Vice President Joe Biden told the press that "I don't think there's any substantive damage, no." The next morning, he announced that "This guy [Assange] has done things that have damaged and put in jeopardy the lives and occupations of other parts of the world." He also called Assange "a high-tech terrorist."

And Manning too became a figure of instant infamy. Rep. Mike Rogers, ranking Republican on the House Intelligence Committee, called the private a traitor who deserved execution. In September, Mike Huckabee, former governor of Arkansas, Baptist pastor and one-time Republican presidential candidate, took a break from signing copies of his new Christmas-themed children's book to recommend execution for Manning.[25]

An ad-hoc nonprofit group, the Bradley Manning Support Network, quickly sprang up. They raised money for Manning and hired an experienced JAG lawyer, David E. Coombs, to defend him. But the detention itself soon came to the fore. Manning's harsh and gratuitous months of punitive solitary confinement at the Quantico brig joined Abu Ghraib and Guantanamo as an emblem of Washington's post-9/11 sadism.

Pretrial confinement in the military justice system is customary only if the accused presents a flight risk or or a risk of harm to self or others. But Pfc. Manning, military authorities decided, was a risk to himself, and this became the pretext for a punishment of extraordinary harshness. Despite the repeated findings of a brig psychiatrist that Manning was not a suicide risk,[26] authorities imposed a regimen of punitive solitary confinement, chillingly described by the accused leaker's attorney:

PFC Manning is currently being held in maximum custody. Since arriving at the Quantico Confinement Facility in July of 2010, he has been held under Prevention of Injury (POI) watch.

His cell is approximately six feet wide and twelve feet in length.

The cell has a bed, a drinking fountain, and a toilet.

The guards at the confinement facility are professional. At no time have they tried to bully, harass, or embarrass PFC Manning. Given the nature of their job, however, they do not engage in conversation with PFC Manning.

At 5:00 A.M. he is woken up (on weekends, he is allowed to sleep until 7:00 A.M.). Under the rules for the confinement facility, he is not allowed to sleep at anytime between 5:00 A.M. and 8:00 P.M. If he attempts to sleep during those hours, he will be made to sit up or stand by the guards.

He is allowed to watch television during the day. The television stations are limited to the basic local stations. His access to the television ranges from 1 to 3 hours on weekdays to 3 to 6 hours on weekends.

He cannot see other inmates from his cell. He can occasionally hear other inmates talk. Due to being a pretrial confinement facility, inmates rarely stay at the facility for any length of time. Currently, there are no other inmates near his cell.

From 7:00 P.M. to 9:20 P.M., he is given correspondence time. He is given access to a pen and paper. He is allowed to write letters to family, friends, and his attorneys.

Each night, during his correspondence time, he is allowed to take a 15 to 20 minute shower.

On weekends and holidays, he is allowed to have approved visitors see him from 12:00 to 3:00 P.M.

He is allowed to receive letters from those on his approved list and from his legal counsel. If he receives a letter from someone not on his approved list, he must sign a rejection form. The letter is then either returned to the sender or destroyed.

He is allowed to have any combination of up to 15 books or magazines. He must request the book or magazine by name. Once the book or magazine has been reviewed by the literary board at the confinement facility, and approved, he is allowed to have someone on his approved list send it to him. The person sending the book or magazine to him must do so through a publisher or an approved distributor such as Amazon. They are not allowed to mail the book or magazine directly to PFC Manning.

Due to being held on Prevention of Injury (POI) watch:

PFC Manning is held in his cell for approximately 23 hours a day.

The guards are required to check on PFC Manning every five minutes by asking him if he is okay. PFC Manning is required to respond in some affirmative manner. At night, if the guards cannot see PFC Manning clearly, because he has a blanket over his head or is curled up towards the wall, they will wake him in order to ensure he is okay.

He receives each of his meals in his cell.

He is not allowed to have a pillow or sheets. However, he is given access to two blankets and has recently been given a new mattress that has a built-in pillow.

He is not allowed to have any personal items in his cell.

He is only allowed to have one book or one magazine at any given time to read in his cell. The book or magazine is taken away from him at the end of the day before he goes to sleep.

He is prevented from exercising in his cell. If he attempts to do push-ups, sit-ups, or any other form of exercise he will be forced to stop.

He does receive one hour of "exercise" outside of his cell daily. He is taken to an empty room and only allowed to walk. PFC Manning normally just walks figure eights in the room for the entire hour. If he indicates that he no longer feels like walking, he is immediately returned to his cell.

When PFC Manning goes to sleep, he is required to strip down to his boxer shorts and surrender his clothing to the guards. His clothing is returned to him the next morning.

Why was Manning treated like the inmate of a Soviet psychiatric prison? Had an American soldier been treated like an enemy combatant? His torture may be a warning to other prospective whistleblowers, and used as a way to break him, crush his spirit and force him to implicate Julian Assange and Wikileaks in espionage charges. (The Department of Justice has had a difficult time finding a legal rationale against Wikileaks, whose act of receiving confidential disclosures is no different from that of the *New York Times* or *Washington Post* in any given week—but if they could get Manning to say that Assange was actively involved in the leaks somehow, they might have a case.)

Manning was kept on POI watch despite month after month of both brig and independent psychiatrists affirming that the prisoner was not a suicide risk. Opposition to his punitive pretrial solitary confinement in the United States and abroad was growing during this time, but Quantico only clamped down harder. In March of 2011, they began stripping Manning naked, depriving him of his glasses as well. The torture and humiliation of the leaker became an even bigger story than the leaks, which at that point included the Iraq War Logs and "Cablegate," the 251,000 State Department cables.

Manning's pretrial torture became an international scandal. British Members of Parliament started protesting the treatment of a Welsh subject's son.[27] The Bundestag's human rights committee sent a letter to Obama expressing concern.[28] Two hundred law professors, including Obama's former mentor Laurence Tribe, wrote an open letter to the president condemning Manning's treatment, if not defending his alleged deeds. (Few are the high-profile American activists and intellectuals who unequivocally defend the leaks: CodePink's core of peace activists, Roseanne Barr, Michael Moore, Jesse Ventura, columnists Jack Shafer and Glenn Greenwald, and Dan Ellsberg himself—but not many more.) Even the hyper-conservative *National Review* blasted the pretrial solitary confinement of Manning as a draconian affront to the rule of law.

On March 10th, State Department spokesperson P. J. Crowley condemned Manning's treatment as "ridiculous and counterproductive and stupid" at an MIT speaking engagement. He resigned two days later.[29]

And where did President Obama stand on this? On the campaign trail, Obama had praised whistleblowers for their patriotism, pledging to protect and promote them. But upon installation in the White House, the Obama Department of Justice launched more Espionage Act prosecutions against leakers than all previous administrations combined. Asked about the issue the day after Crowley's outburst, Obama reassured the reporter that he personally looked into the matter and that the months of pretrial solitary confinement were all for the soldier's own good. Confronted by a group of Manning solidarity activists, who thanks to a benefactor had infiltrated a $5,000-a-plate fundraiser for the President at the St. Regis Hotel in San Francisco, Barack Obama informed them with exasperation that Bradley Manning "broke the law. I can't do open source diplomacy!"[30]

If Manning were so abused by the Bush-Cheney gang, it would have been one more proof of the Republicans' noisome barbarity. But with Obama in office, Democrats have been remarkably mellow about the matter—save, of course, those Obama loyalists who have aggressively condemned Manning's alleged deeds, mocked his defenders and praised his incarceration as essential to national security.

It's tempting to figure that Manning's sexual preference and gender identity played a large role in his alleged deeds. A young sensitive gay man, alienated and brutalized by the Army's macho culture—it makes some intuitive sense. It is a temptation worth resisting, as it is not supported by any of the available evidence. The informant who turned Manning in is gay, as is the former Army counterintelligence special agent, Tim Webster, whom Lamo first turned to after receiving the alleged confession from FOB Hammer, and who then connected Lamo with the military authorities. Webster told *The Guardian* he had no time whatsoever for the fixation on Manning's sexuality. "The notion that the Manning case has anything to do with his sexuality is categorically absurd. Many thousands of homosexual and bisexual men and women are serving honorably and to suggest that their sexuality renders them any less effective in the defense of our nation is bigoted nonsense." There are thousands of gays and lesbians in the military, many with security clearance, and they have been largely happy to obey all their orders, both legal and illegal, and would never dream of doing what Manning is alleged to have done.

Manning himself never linked his sexual preference or gender identity to his alleged deeds. In fact, the way he described the military, it seems a virtual magnet for gays and lesbians. There was the colonel that Manning had a fling with back when he was a Starbucks barista in Maryland; the interrogator at FOB Hammer who was in a civil union back in New Jersey; the claim that "half the S-2 shop [military intelligence unit] is at least bi."

(It should also be pointed out that some of the most bellicose politicians on both sides of the Atlantic are rumored to be gay. The South Carolina chapter of the Tea Party has delightedly outed again and again their über-hawkish but otherwise insufficiently conservative senator, Lindsey Graham, as a homosexual. Liam Fox, the recently resigned minister of defense in the Tory-Liberal Democrat government in the United Kingdom, is a neocon ultra who carried out his official duties abroad very frequently in the company of his "best friend," a man seventeen years his junior without any governmental position but bankrolled as a "consultant" by various wealthy individuals close to Fox.)

In the United States, mainstream LGBT activists have been more than happy to shun Manning; with the Don't Ask Don't Tell policy of prohibiting "out" gays and lesbians from the military finally and triumphantly repealed, why defend an accused traitor who just happens to be gay? In the United Kingdom, where the LGBT rights movement is less beholden to the military, the mood is different and leading gay rights and human rights activist Peter Tatchell has promoted solidarity with Manning (he of the Welsh mother) at every opportunity.

Whistleblowers are always pathologized; their governments refuse on principle to comprehend their political motive, no matter how overt and obvious. In the United States, we are barely able to even comprehend a political motive, given that the whole category of the political has eroded so severely, fatally associated with the ghastly talking heads who appear on Sunday morning talk shows. Despite the clarity of Manning's stated *mens rea* in the chatlogs, a political motive simply won't do. His motive must be sexual, as we have seen. Or it must be emotional. (As if Bradley Manning, who was dumped by his boyfriend in January of 2010, is somehow different from the thousands of other soldiers and sailors similarly jilted every year.) It must be psychiatric. (That mental illness is rampant throughout the armed forces is rarely mentioned, nor the fact that the leading cause of death among active duty troops in 2009, 2010 and 2011 is not enemy fire or IEDs but suicide.) It must be pharmacological. (According to the *Washington Post*, Dr. David Charney, a psychiatrist who has consulted on espionage cases, pointed out that Manning's reported tendencies to zone out might be related to "petit mal epilepsy."[31]) So much concern, such eagerness to diagnose.

The irony is that Manning himself in his IM chats with Lamo already dismissed the pathologization of every last personality trait.

(01:51:59 AM) bradass87: im probably suffering from depression
(01:51:59 AM) bradass87: ={
(01:52:03 AM) bradass87: ={
(01:52:06 AM) bradass87: =P
(01:52:15 AM) info@adrianlamo.com: Who isn't :(
(01:52:20 AM) bradass87: goddamn, i missed the "P" key twice
(01:52:27 AM) info@adrianlamo.com: I'm supposedly bipolar.
(01:52:38 AM) bradass87: oh well, still not medicated

(01:53:00 AM) bradass87: i dont believe a third of the DSM-IV-TR

(01:53:58 AM) bradass87: so many Disorders that so many people fall into... it just seems like a method to categorize a person, medicate them, and make money from prescription medications

[...]

(01:54:31 AM) bradass87: i'd like to meet a single person that wouldn't fall into a Disorder in the DSM-IV-TR

And yet, most media accounts of Manning and his alleged deeds have made a meal of the private's personal life and do not even go near his plainly stated motive. Commentator Joy Reid, a Harvard-educated blogger, commentator and Obama loyalist is typical in this regard, seeing Manning as "a guy seeking anarchy as a salve for his own personal, psychological torment." Reid also says Manning's "gender identity disorder" "kind of puts his subsequent terms of incarceration in context."[32] Meaning that it's okay to lock transgender people in solitary for as long as you want? The comment is certainly open to interpretation.

Is the political angle too obvious for clever journalists? One man with no patience for the media's lurid fixation on Manning's personal life is Ethan McCord—the US infantryman who retrieved the two wounded children from the shot-up van on July 12, 2007, all filmed between the cross-hairs in the "Collateral Murder" video. He responded to a *New York Magazine* article on Manning that dwelt at length on the soldier's gender identity counseling, but barely mentioned his crisis of conscience after helping to round up Iraqi civilian activists for likely torture. McCord's cogent letter to *New York* is worth quoting in full, even if the magazine printed only a snippet.

Serving with my unit 2nd battalion 16th infantry in New Baghdad, Iraq, I vividly remember the moment in 2007, when our Battalion

Commander walked into the room and announced our new rules of engagement:

"Listen up, new battalion SOP (standing operating procedure) from now on: Anytime your convoy gets hit by an IED, I want 360 degree rotational fire. You kill every [expletive] in the street!"

We weren't trained extensively to recognize an unlawful order, or how to report one. But many of us could not believe what we had just been told to do. Those of us who knew it was morally wrong struggled to figure out a way to avoid shooting innocent civilians, while also dodging repercussions from the non-commissioned officers who enforced the policy. In such situations, we determined to fire our weapons, but into rooftops or abandoned vehicles, giving the impression that we were following procedure.

On April 5, 2010 American citizens and people around the world got a taste of the fruits of this standing operating procedure when Wikileaks [1] released the now-famous Collateral Murder [2] video. This video showed the horrific and wholly unnecessary killing of unarmed Iraqi civilians and Reuters journalists.

I was part of the unit that was responsible for this atrocity. In the video, I can be seen attempting to carry wounded children to safety in the aftermath.

The video released by Wikileaks belongs in the public record. Covering up this incident is a matter deserving of criminal inquiry. Whoever revealed it is an American hero in my book.

Private First Class Bradley Manning has been confined for over a year on the government's accusation that he released this video and volumes of other classified documents to Wikileaks—an organization that has been selectively publishing portions of this information in collaboration with other news outlets.

If PFC Bradley Manning did what he is accused of doing, then it is clear—from chat logs [3] that have been attributed to him—that his decision was motivated by conscience and political agency. These chat logs allegedly describe how PFC Manning hopes these revelations will result in "worldwide discussion, debates, and reforms."

Unfortunately, Steve Fishman's article Bradley Manning's Army of One [4] in *New York Magazine* (July 3, 2011) erases Manning's political agency. By focusing so heavily on Manning's personal life, Fishman removes politics from a story that has everything to do with politics. The important public issues wrapped up with PFC Manning's case include: transparency in government; the Obama Administration's unprecedented pursuit of whistle-blowers; accountability of government and military in shaping and carrying out foreign policy; war crimes revealed in the Wikileaks documents; the catalyzing role these revelations played in democratic movements across the Middle East; and more.

The contents of the Wikileaks revelations have pulled back the curtain on the degradation of our democratic system. It has become completely normal for decision-makers to promulgate foreign policies, diplomatic strategies, and military operating procedures that are hostile to the democratic ideals our country was founded upon. The incident I was part of—shown in the Collateral Murder video—becomes even more horrific when we grasp that it was not exceptional. PFC Manning himself is alleged to describe (in the chat logs) an incident where he was ordered to turn over innocent Iraqi academics to notorious police interrogators, for the offense of publishing a political critique of government corruption titled, "Where did the money go? [5]" These issues deserve "discussion, debates, and reforms"—and attention from journalists.

Fishman's article was also ignorant of the realities of military service. Those of us who serve in the military are often lauded as heroes.

Civilians need to understand that we may be heroes, but we are not saints. We are young people under a tremendous amount of stress. We face moral dilemmas that many civilians have never even contemplated hypothetically.

Civil society honors military service partly because of the sacrifice it entails. Lengthy and repeated deployments stress our closest relationships with family and friends. The realities, traumas, and stresses of military life take an emotional toll. This emotional battle is part of the sacrifice that we honor. That any young soldier might wrestle with his or her experiences in the military, or with his or her identity beyond military life, should never be wielded as a weapon against them.

If PFC Bradley Manning did what he is accused of, he is a hero of mine; not because he's perfect or because he never struggled with personal or family relationships—most of us do—but because in the midst of it all he had the courage to act on his conscience.[33]

An unlikely hero? No doubt. In the as-yet unauthenticated chatlogs, Manning recognizes that status as a gay, soon-to-be transgender atheist unsuits him thoroughly to be a poster-child for the cause of transparent government: "[I']m way way way too easy to marginalize[.]"

And yet that is just what he has become all over the world: a poster child for the cause of honest dealing, patriotic dissent, and the right to know what one's government is doing. He is a global icon and source of inspiration. Bradley Manning solidarity groups are all over the world. A Germany radical group has been vandalizing the national railroads, calling for the pullout of German troops from Afghanistan—and for the release of Bradley Manning. (Wikileaks, by the way, has condemned these acts of sabotage.) Larbi Sadiki, a Tunisian-born sociologist who teaches in the UK, tells me that Manning will surely be remembered as a great man of conscience, a liberator of valuable knowledge. "I don't want to exaggerate his importance, but the story of the Tunisian revolution really cannot be told without his contribution of those State Department cables." Tony Jean-Thenor, leader of a Haitian grassroots community group in South Florida, says that "Manning will never die anymore; he'll be alive for generations for what he did to help not only Haitians but oppressed people all over the world. History will exonerate him."[34]

Brig regulations bar anyone who didn't have some prior relationship with Manning from coming to visit him in person: the scribblers and camera crews have been kept at bay. Manning's lawyer has apparently advised his client to keep his mouth shut before the court martial, in the interests of strategic prudence. The UN special rapporteur continues to be denied unsupervised access, as required by the Convention Against Torture, ratified by the United States in 1994. Even so, Bradley Manning has never been more connected to the world. According to his lawyer, Manning gets hundreds of letters from all over the world every week, for which the prisoner is most grateful.

No account of Bradley Manning can omit an account of his alleged leaks: their context, their content and their reception.

3

THE LEAKS

(1:11:54 PM) **bradass87:** and... its important that it gets out... i feel, for some bizarre reason

(1:12:02 PM) **bradass87:** it might actually change something

The Afghan War Logs, the Iraq War Logs, the Guantánamo files, the State Department Cables: this is what the fuss is all about, why Manning is viewed as a tragic patriot and hero by some, by others as a traitor. My quick perusal of Manning's alleged disclosures will start with a study of the context of the leaks: the measures that Washington does and does not take to control information, and whether these steps actually secure information or are merely theatrical. Second, we will survey the leaks themselves, their content and their meaning. Finally, I will examine the reception of the leaks, both in the United States and abroad. At every step it will become apparent that the logic of secrecy and security in twenty-first-century United States is anything but straightforward.

I. The Context

Washington expends enormous effort to control the information it generates—through hair-trigger classification of official documents, the censorship of government employees and the aggressive prosecution of whistleblowers. At the very same time, Washington condones any number of leaks from elite officials who make no secret of their illegal disclosures. As for the national security state's data security apparatus, though expanding and costly, it is dysfunctional: incontinent and constantly sloshing classified material. This conflicting set of policies and impulses can be described as paradoxical, and though paradox, at the level of pure ideas, can be charming, at the level of giant bureaucracies the term denotes chaos. In fact the bizarre combination of lackadaisical security, punitive response and official hypocrisy make the nation's information security regime a macrocosm of the Manning affair itself.

First, Washington's habit of classifying public documents goes well beyond the protection of legitimate state secrets like nuclear launch codes. Instead, the federal agencies tend to mark every last public record even tangentially related to military and diplomatic policy as a state secret of some degree of confidentiality. Because the total of such documents is so astronomically high, no precise figure exists. According to the Information Security Oversight Office, the federal agency tasked with maintaining information security, officials classified nearly seventy-seven million documents in 2010. and ninety-two million in 2011.[1]

What are the consequences to public discourse of such rampant over-classification? The question is not new. James Madison wrote, "a popular government, without popular information, is but a prelude to a tragedy or farce, or perhaps both." And though the nation's fourth president could not have envisioned the modern administrative state or an American military presence in over a hundred foreign nations we can also be sure that Madison would never have foreseen that documents from his own presidency would, over two hundred years later, still be locked away as state secrets. And yet it was only in the middle of 2011 that the National Security Agency got around to declassifying a cache of military documents dating to 1809, the first year of Madison's presidency.[2] Declassification seems to occur at a geological tempo: the CIA still keeps documents from the First World War classified, and only in 2010 released records from the failed Bay of Pigs invasion.[3]

Diplomatic historians, who serve as an indispensable repository of national memory, complain bitterly about the gratuitous, reflexive and often apparently irrational classification and redaction of public records. Others have criticized the current regime of over-classification, which leads inevitably to a kind of self-willed societal dementia, as a national security liability. "Secret programs stifled public debate on the decisions that shaped our response to the September 11 attacks," notes a report by the Brennan Center for Justice at NYU Law School.[4] "The classification system must be reformed if we are to preserve the critical role that transparent government plays in a functioning democracy." At the operational level of national security, routinized secrecy also prevents the access of law-enforcement agencies to sought-after information. Coleen Rowley, a longtime FBI special agent and attorney who was one of *Time* magazine's three persons of the year in 2002, has even editorialized that an outlet like Wikileaks might have averted the 9/11 attacks by providing FBI and other law enforcement agents with a forum to share urgent information still classified by our baroque security bureaucracy.[5]

There is, not surprisingly, a dawning consensus among the elite that the federal government's classification regime has become less a sensible precaution than a mania. "Depending on who you ask, over-classification is either very widespread or extremely widespread," says

Steven Aftergood, an expert on government secrecy at the Federation of American Scientists. "Everybody from the director of national intelligence to President Obama has acknowledged the problem."[6] And the Obama administration has even taken some small steps to remedy the problem: in his first year in office, he issued an executive order that created the National Declassification Center to deal with the backlog of over 400 million classified documents; a year later the President signed the Reducing Over-Classification Act passed in late 2010.

But the effect of these measures has been minimal. Although the Department of Defense has scrapped 82 of its classification guides, this is only 4% of the 1,878 total.[7] The 77 million classified documents tabulated for 2010 is a 40% increase over the year before—though government officials say this is because of tighter reporting guidelines. J. William Leonard, director of the federal Information Security Oversight Office from 2002 to 2007, has said that federal agencies need to start sanctioning officials who over-classify in order to prevent secrecy from becoming the default option for bureaucrats lacking any incentive to make documents publicly available.[8] One thing is certain: until a new ethic of transparency is spliced into the DNA of every federal agency, over-classification will continue to distort and stifle public debate on vital issues of war and statecraft.

The government has also sought to restrict the release of information through censorship of former officials and the aggressive prosecution of whistleblowers.

Government censorship has enjoyed a robust revival since the autumn of 2001. Veteran FBI agent Ali Soufan was surprised to find that information he had read into the public record at Congressional hearings, including facts readily available in the official 9/11 report, was now deemed a threat to national security and expunged from his memoir.[9] As Scott Shane of the *New York Times* noted, the government's censorship "amounts to a fight over who gets to write the history of the September 11 attacks and their aftermath."[10] This is not an isolated case. Peter Van Buren, the Foreign Service officer who was a contemporary of Bradley Manning's at FOB Hammer, found that the publication of his memoir of leading a civilian reconstruction team in Iraq got him stripped of his security clearance and placed on administrative leave—though the official pretext was his linking to a WikiLeak'ed State Department cable on his personal blog. On some occasions, publishers have held fast in the face of government demands for withdrawal of the book, as with Henry Holt's refusal to suppress Van Buren's memoir in the face of federal pressure. When the government is more alert, however, it is liable to buy up an entire print run of a newly published book, as it did in 2010 with former Lt. Col Anthony Shaffer's memoir of his half-year in Afghanistan as a Defense Intelligence Agency officer.[11] Of course more than 200 review copies are still at large, and many of the redactions to the first edition were of facts easily found online. "This is a book that hardly anybody would have read, and now it's poised to become a best seller," said Steven Aftergood of the Federation of American Scientists. "The smart move would have been to do nothing."[12]

As for the prosecution of insiders who expose government wrongdoing, it has reached a new vindictive intensity in the Obama administration. Although candidate Obama campaigned as the whistleblower's loyal friend and protector, he has presided over more leaks prosecutions under the Espionage Act of 1917—a use that the statute's authors never intended—than all his predecessors combined. The most perverse of these has been the aggressive prosecution of former National Security Agency official Thomas Drake, who informed a reporter at the Baltimore *Sun* of the colossal waste, fraud and illegality of the NSA's warrantless wiretapping program. The government accused him of ten felonies with a maximum penalty of 35 years, only to withdraw all the gravest charges just days before the trial. The prosecution settled for a plea bargain, with Drake copping to a misdemeanor based on his possession at home of a confidential email which the government had retroactively classified *after* it was discovered. ("I've never seen a more deliberate and willful example of government officials improperly classifying a document," said J. William Leonard, former head of the ISOO.[13]) Judge Richard D. Bennett, appointed to the federal bench by George W. Bush, blasted the prosecution for putting defendant Drake through "four years of hell" and coming up with an indictment that ultimately "doesn't pass the smell test."[14] (Prosecutor William Welch II had also seen his corruption case against former Alaska Senator Ted Stevens collapse, an overreach also excoriated by a federal judge, but there is apparently no consequence for overzealous prosecutions in our Department of Justice.)

Since 9/11, the national security apparatus was disbursed near-unlimited funding, resulting in an elephantiasis-like expansion of state apparatuses intended to ensure the control of information. One might easily assume that, given these expensive and often zealous efforts, Washington must now command a hermetically sealed information security regime. One would be wrong. Despite this spasmodic gesturing at secrecy, Washington, in the words of former Secretary of Defense Robert Gates, "leaks like a sieve and always has."[15] There are two ways that Washington regularly sluices classified information: intentionally and unintentionally.

First, the intentional sort. Leaks, far from being an unspeakable taboo in Washington, are an accepted and thoroughly routine medium of communication between elite officials and their preferred journalists. As pundit Glenn Greenwald frequently points out, in any given week "unnamed sources" will reveal to the media such matters as the role of

Russia's security services in bombing an embassy in neighboring Georgia; the violent misdeeds of Pakistan's Inter-Service Intelligence Agency; the progress of the military campaign against the Libyan government—all sensitive matters relating to ongoing wars or relations with great powers or critical allies.[16] Yet such leaks of material classed as top secret—a higher classification than anything allegedly released by Pfc. Manning— never register as security risks or even as leaks—they are business as usual: another *Washington Post* story citing "unnamed officials"; another Sy Hersh piece in the *New Yorker*; the latest Bob Woodward book. Such leaking is never denied; in fact it's a source of bonhomous hilarity between elite media and officialdom. In a revealing conversation with the website *Politico*, Obama's chief of staff William Daley discussed his predecessor Rahm Emanuel's propensity to leak.

> Rahm was famous for calling reporters, do you call reporters? I ask.
>
> "I call; I'm not as aggressive leaking and stroking," Daley says. "I'm not reflecting on Rahm, but I'm not angling for something else, you know? Rahm is a lot younger [Emmanuel is 51], and he knew he was going to be doing something else in two years or four years or eight years, and I'm in a different stage. I'm not going to become the leaker in chief."
>
> You've got others for that, I say.
>
> "Yeah, and hopefully in some organized leaking fashion," Daley says, laughing. "I'm all for leaking when it's organized."[17]

The government's winking half-disclosure of certain actions and protocols—for instance, the use of CIA drones to assassinate American citizen al-Awlaki—can be almost virtuosic in the way it takes credit for controversial policy while refusing any accountability. Though the faux-secrecy surrounding the Awlaki assassination did raise some eyebrows, Washington's embedded media corps generally finds the official coyness on such matters to be not problematic but adorable.

Even beyond these intentional leaks, it turns out that the security apparatus itself is anything but an airtight vessel. The institutional landscape of the secrecy regime is in chaos. With the federal budget ballooning for the sixteen national security agencies, it is not clear who is responsible for what, and whether any institution has any overarching authority at all. National security journalist Dana Priest of the *Washington Post* has found that many of the high officials had no idea even what many of the initials of their sister-agencies stood for.[18] (The Director of National Intelligence, a newfangled cabinet-level position, is supposed to supervise all intelligence agencies but in real life he or she does not, leading its third director, retired admiral Dennis Blair to quit in May, 2010.) This quasi-anarchic network of bureaucracies, with no centralized oversight, not only leaks; it hemorrhages information. Rick Wallace, a researcher at Tiversa, a data protection firm in Pennsylvania, and a private citizen who holds no security clearance, showed Priest some of the classified items he had found on the internet: a 2010 top secret Intelligence Summary of Afghanistan; TSA documents detailing the places on an airplane that are not usually searched, classified records from every wing of the Department of Homeland Security.[19] How is this possible? For one, 850,000 individuals hold a top-secret security clearance today, begging the question of how "secret" such broadly accessible information really is to begin with. And as Priest points out, "the managers of Top Secret America, who range in age from forty-five to sixty-five years old [...] may not be conversant with the simplest technologies of the information era." File-sharing software like Gnutella that many officials do not understand—but is often installed on their laptops by their children—routinely makes top-secret material available to anyone who is looking.[20] Despite astronomical expenditures—the annual cost of securing "national security" information according to William Bosanko, director of the Information Security Oversight office, is $10 billion—the information security apparatus of the United States government is a leaky mess.[21]

The purpose of this is not to spread alarms about vital secrets being lost—given how rampant the current hair-trigger classification scheme works, this is hardly likely. It is rather to point out that current classification regime is a tragic, bloated farce—the SCIF at FOB Hammer writ enormous, and expensive. It is entirely reasonable to question what purpose these intelligence agencies serve. Despite the colossal resources and focus on the Arab world, these agencies failed completely to see the "Arab Spring" coming just as the CIA failed to see the sudden collapse of the Warsaw Pact and then Soviet Union two decades earlier.

We might add that the security of information in the military is also a thoroughly leaky system. Evan Knappenberger is, like Manning, a graduate of the Army's Fort Huachuca intelligence training school who later served in Iraq. According to him, the lax to nonexistent information security that Pfc. Manning found at FOB Hammer is no outlier.

Army security is like a Band-Aid on a sunken chest wound. I remember when I was training, before I had my clearance even, they were talking about diplomatic cables. It was a big scandal at Fort Huachuca (Arizona), with all these kids from analyst school. Somebody said (in the cables) Saddam wanted to negotiate and was willing to agree to peace terms before we invaded, and Bush said no. And this wasn't very widely known. Somehow it came across on a cable at Fort Huachuca, and everybody at the fort knew about it.

It's interesting the access we had. I did the briefing for a two-star general every morning for a year. So I had secret and top-secret information readily available. The funny thing is, [Western Washington State College]'s password system they have here on all these computers is better security than the Army had on their secret computers.

There are 2 million people, many of them not US citizens, with access to SIPRNet [Secret Internet Protocol Router Network, the Department of Defense's largest network for the exchange of classified information and messages]. There are 1,400 government agencies with SIPR websites. It's not that secret.[22]

Knappenberger also alleges that the US military had made SIPRNet accessible to the Iraqi military, in full knowledge that the body contained many actors engaged in covert hostilities against occupying forces.[23] (Knappenberger has praised Pfc. Bradley Manning's alleged deeds as principled and entirely beneficial, pointing out that American civilians very much need to know what their wars are all about.) The conclusion is clear: the nation's information security regime is only FOB Hammer's SCIF writ large, an expensive non-secure apparatus containing millions of non-secrets, erratically punctuated with bizarre and unreasonable punishments for whistleblowers who don't break the law properly.

It seems to have been easy to get and disseminate the Wikileaks caches. What is truly worrisome, then, is that no one until Private Manning saw fit to disclose these public documents, so many of which have been vital to the public discourse—particularly in the United States. We will now turn to the leaks themselves.

II. The Content

Given the international furor over Bradley Manning's pretrial torture, his heroic (if polarizing) personal story, the distinctly Stieg Larsson/ Mission Impossible flavor of the whole Wikileaks enterprise, not to mention the unrelated legal travails of Julian Assange in both Sweden and Great Britain, the leaks themselves have almost been swallowed up by the story *of* the leaks. To winch the leaks from their own self-referential morass, we will briefly survey the four major caches that have added so much to the world's understanding of twenty-first-century statecraft.

On July 25, 2010, the *New York Times*, *Der Spiegel* and *The Guardian* began reporting on, and releasing, some 92,000 confidential field reports from the Afghan War, all dating between January 2004 and December 2009. The War Diary made some 75,000 documents available, with some 15,000 retained by Wikileaks for closer review and redaction, lest they put Afghan civilians named in the logs at risk. The field-log panorama offered by these documents reveal a brutal pacification campaign with only a distant resemblance to the philanthropic nation-building described in the press releases of the International Security Assistance Forces (ISAF).

A few highlights:

- The activities of Task Force 373, an elite corps not integrated into ISAF, and their mission to kill or capture those named on their Joint Prioritized Effects List (JPEL). In other words, a hit list. In the course of dispatching those listed, Task Force 373 has killed civilians, among them seven children in the rubble of a school targeted as an insurgent hideout on June 17, 2007.[24]
- The potted history of Combat Outpost Keating, isolated in Nuristan Province in northeastern Afghanistan near the Pakistan border. The logs record that local Afghans who worked with the soldiers were often brutally murdered, and that the insurgents (Taliban or otherwise) had firm control over the area by 2009. In October of that year, at least 175 armed insurgents assaulted the outpost in a nine-hour firefight that killed eight US soldiers and wounded dozens, with Afghan casualties less scrupulously recorded. The

author of the report editorializes that the story of Combat Outpost Keating is the Afghan war in microcosm.[25]

- One hundred forty-four incidents in which coalition forces killed civilians, including twenty-one instances of British troops attacking civilians.[26]
- The widespread suspicion, voiced in some 180 field logs though never proven, that Pakistan's intelligence agency is in cahoots with the Taliban, providing them a cross-border haven as well as material support.[27]

Although the mosaic of these field reports offers no focal point as horrifically mediagenic as the Collateral Murder video, their cumulative impact is stark. (The documents relating to the Granai massacre, which according to the Afghan government killed some 150 people, were deleted from Wikileaks' data hoard by a disgruntled former deputy of Julian Assange.) The Afghanistan war described in these suppressed records is a pacification campaign replete with civilian deaths and friendly fire, all perched unsteadily on the shakiest geostrategic footing. As of this writing, President Karzai is begging ISAF to cease its night raids into Afghan villages while Pakistan has closed its supply routes in retaliation for American troops shooting dead 24 Pakistani troops on Pakistan's side of the border on November 26, 2011.

The Iraq War Logs were released on October 22, 2010, in partnership with *Der Spiegel*, *Le Monde*, Al Jazeera, *The Guardian*, the *New York Times*, the Bureau of Investigative Journalism and the Iraq Body Count Project. These 391,832 documents, each a "Significant Action" field log, provide a synoptic image of the war from 2004 through 2009; together they are the largest leak of military documents to date. Among the highlights:

- The Collateral Murder video (released in April 2010 as a kind of preview to the Iraq material), a gunsight view of Apache helicopters opening fire on a small group of Iraqis, most of them unarmed civilians and two of them Reuters News Agency employees, on the streets of a Baghdad suburb April 2007.[28]

- An estimate of civilian deaths, whose existence the Pentagon had repeatedly denied. The figure is put at 109,000, among whom 66,081 are civilians, which includes "hundreds" of civilians killed at US military checkpoints. The Iraq Body Count project used these records to add 15,000 new deaths to its tally, reaching a total of some 150,000, of which 80% were civilians.[29]

- Documentation of a house raid by US forces in which American soldiers summarily executed one man, four women, two children and three infants. The cable includes an excerpt from a letter of inquiry by the United Nations' Special Rapporteur on Extrajudicial Executions. A US airstrike was launched to destroy the house, but "autopsies carried out at the Tikrit Hospital's morgue revealed that all corpses were shot in the head and handcuffed." This leak received wide media attention in Iraq and was a major factor behind the Iraqi government's insistence that US forces only be allowed to stay if they lose immunity to the domestic law of Iraq.[30]

- Widespread torture by Iraqi authorities, including sexual torture, cutting off fingers, acid burns and fatal beatings. The leaks also reveal the existence of "Fragmentary Order 242," an order for the US military to ignore acts of Iraqi torture despite the public admonition of the Chairman of the Joint Chiefs of Staff Peter Pace that it was the duty of every occupying American troop to prevent such behavior wherever they saw it.[31]

At the beginning of the Obama presidency, the prison at Guantánamo Bay, whose officials still gamely call it a "detention facility," was proof of Bush–Cheney illegalities. Three years later, Gitmo is a normalized feature of American national security policy, one that Democratic voters try very hard to ignore. But the "Guantánamo Files" that Wikileaks released on April 25, 2011 through the *Washington Post* and the British Daily *Telegraph* made it harder for the world to wish this military prison away. The 759 "detainee assessment" dossiers, spanning 2002 to 2009 and covering all but twenty prisoners, shine a searching, revealing light into a legal black hole.[32]

Some background: though Cheney claimed that the Gitmo prisoners were the "worst of the worst," by the end of 2008, the Bush Administration had already released nearly 600 of the inmates for lack of any evidence that they were a threat. (As the US military purchased Afghanistan-based terrorists for a generous bounty, local militias were less than scrupulous about whom they rounded up; the documents show that some half of the 212 Afghan prisoners sent to Gitmo were either Shanghaied by local armed groups or forced into fighting by other local groups.) Of the 171 prisoners that remain at Guantánamo—each at a cost of $800,000 per year—eighty-nine have been cleared for release while a few dozen have been marked for indefinite detention. The evidence collected against this group is deemed credible by the military authorities, but was extracted by torture, an embarrassment to the US government in any court proceeding.

The Gitmo files bring much into focus: tenuous relationships with other intelligence services; delicate geopolitical dances; the sloppily indiscriminate round-up of prisoners—and most of all, the individual prisoners. The story of Al Jazeera cameraman Sami al-Hajj, a Sudanese first thought to be an al-Qaeda courier, but kept at Gitmo for seven years apparently to learn the ins and outs of his employer, seen by

Washington as insufficiently pro-American in its broadcasts. The story of Abdul Badr Mannon, a Pakistani journalist handed over by Pakistan's Inter-Service Intelligence, whom the US interrogators later came to believe was rounded up because he was uncovering ties between Muslim radicals and the Pakistani state.[33] (The files specify that a prisoner's links to the ISI should be just as troublesome as a tie to al-Qaeda.) In age the prisoners ranged from fourteen-year-old Naqib Ullah, to an eighty-nine-year-old, Mohammed Sadiq, already in his dotage, health failing.

Defense lawyers representing various prisoners may still not admit any of the dossiers' content as evidence. These documents, though available from any uncensored internet signal, laughably remain an official state secret.

Thanks to Wikileaks and to the journalists who have sifted through these vital documents—particularly Carol Rosenberg of McClatchy/ Knight Ridder, dean of the Gitmo correspondents, and relentless blogger and author Andy Worthington—we now have a far clearer picture of what is now an enduring American institution. (We will return to Guantánamo in Chapter Four.) We can only hope that Wikileaks will next expose the inner workings of Bagram Prison in Afghanistan, Gitmo's larger "evil twin" holding 2,400 prisoners, some 400 of whom were recommended for release by General Petraeus himself before his move to the CIA. As of this writing, those 400 prisoners have not been freed.[34]

Wikileaks began releasing 251,287 US State Department cables on November 28, 2010, in collaboration with *El País, Der Spiegel, The Guardian*, the *New York Times* and other media outlets whose staff redacted the documents to minimize any risk to individuals named in the files. Of the total, 15,652 are "secret," 101,748 are "confidential" and the rest—more than half—unclassified. On September 1, 2011, Wikileaks made the whole cache available and under the coordination of the organization, the database of cables was "crowdsourced" to accelerate the sifting of the dump. Almost oceanic in volume and geographical scope—274 embassies—the cables are too vast to explore in any depth here. Many summaries and highlights have already been compiled, but we will quickly survey the diplomatic cables to highlight some critical zones of interest.

Many of the cables are candid letters back to Washington about local conditions: sobering dispatches from Italy's efforts against organized crime in Calabria and Sicily; an account of a Dagestani wedding in the Russian Caucasus that is a minor masterpiece of travel writing. But many of the leaked cables have more than entertainment value and have been eagerly seized on by the peoples of various nations who see the US embassy as a reliable source of information. In the Dominican Republic, the national government has shed dozens of highly compensated but not particularly useful "vice-ministers" after leaked criticism in a US cable;[35] the Guyanese press has also thanked Wikileaks for helping to expose governmental corruption.[36]

The most famous instance of this is in Tunisia, where the leaked assessments of the US ambassador—candidly unflattering accounts of the corruption and greed of the ruling Ben Ali clan and hangers-on— added fuel to the fire of discontent that led Tunisians to overthrow their longstanding authoritarian government.

Other cables are less flattering to the United States and show Washington willing to trample a great many values in pursuit of idiosyncratically defined security goals in both counter-terror policy and in various American wars.

The cables reveal how the US government exerted heavy pressure to suppress a German criminal investigation into the CIA kidnapping of Khaled El-Masri, an innocent Germany citizen mistakenly identified as a terror suspect who was abducted and then rendered to Afghanistan for extensive torture.[37] The cables also reveal similar US arm-twisting to thwart a Spanish investigation into a similar case.

The United States has endeavored mightily to have its multiplying wars be designated "just wars" or at least not denounced as unjust. The manner in which Washington seeks this end is not by careful consideration of the use of military force but by forceful lobbying at the Vatican, whose verdict on all matters of "just war" carries immense political clout worldwide. The leaks reveal much worldly retail politicking done by both the Holy See and the US ambassador, and rather less in the way of disinterested *caritas*.[38]

The most worthwhile cables, as well as the most sordid, describe America's support for various authoritarian and semi-democratic client states in the Middle East. We learn, for instance, that the Crown Prince of Bahrain studied military science at Fort Leavenworth—where Bradley Manning has been incarcerated since April 2011. We also learn that Egypt—second-largest recipient of American foreign aid in the past three decades—has sent its notoriously torture-using security forces to Quantico, Virginia for interrogation training at FBI headquarters. Needless to say, training for an authoritarian government's security forces reveals Washington's "freedom agenda" for the Middle East to be so much drivel.

The leaks also provide a window into military and diplomatic relations with Israel, for decades the top recipient of US foreign aid. The cables reveal the diplomatic efforts to keep quiet the provision of "Bunker Buster" bombs to Israel, lest they trigger speculation about a strike on Iran;[39] the regular briefing of US diplomats as to the humanitarian crisis in Gaza, which Israel intended to "keep functioning at the lowest level possible consistent with avoiding a humanitarian crisis";[40] the unedifying sight of Michael Posner, formerly head of Human Rights First and now Assistant Secretary of State for Human Rights and Labor, helping the Israeli government downplay the atrocities they committed in their 2008–2009 assault on Gaza.[41]

Leaks transferred to the *Nation* magazine and *Haïti Liberté* revealed that when the Haitian government moved to raise the hourly minimum wage from 22 cents to 61 cents, the US State Department, in close concert with Hanes, Fruit of the Loom and Levi-Strauss, strong-armed the Haitians into carving out an exemption for the multinational textile makers.[42] Haiti is the poorest nation in the Americas and one third of its people are, in the artful term favored by the Third-World development industry, "food insecure."

Another recurring theme is the pressure exerted by large pharmaceutical firms on US foreign policy. With emerging markets providing the largest growth area for pharmaceutical sales, Big Pharma is desperate to export the favorable intellectual property regulatory framework that ensures monopolistic sales with no cheaply made competitors, guaranteeing high prices and high profits. The push to adopt an American-style regulatory framework to the benefit of Big Pharma comes up in cables from Poland, France, India and elsewhere. According to James Love, director of the advocacy group Knowledge Ecology International, "All the things the US is doing is whatever benefits a handful of companies like Pfizer, Abbott, Merck, and so on. The US basically pushes for anything they want."[43]

A cache of cables reveal the jockeying among foreign ministries to facilitate the exploitation of natural resources within the Arctic circle. As the ice cap melts, instead of taking concerted action to halt global warming there is an apparent scrum to clinch access to the region's vast gas and oil reserves. According to Ben Ayliffe of Greenpeace, "Instead of seeing the melting of the Arctic ice cap as a spur to action on climate change, the leaders of the Arctic nations are instead investing in military hardware to fight for the oil beneath it. They're preparing to fight to extract the very fossil fuels that caused the melting in the first place. It's like pouring gasoline on fire."[44]

In all cases, it is difficult to discern how the State Department's actions, though perhaps effective as corporate lobbying, actually serve the interests of the American people, the great majority of whom are not owners of preferred stock in Merck or hangers-on of the Mubarak family. It is also difficult to approve of the directive, signed both by Hillary Clinton and her predecessor, Condoleezza Rice, that US diplomats collect DNA samples, fingerprints and biometric information, credit card numbers, passport and frequent flyer IDs from other diplomats at the United Nations.[45]

III. The Reception of the Leaks

The gift of Wikileaks has not been well received in the United States. Yet no other country stands as much to gain from the disclosures. With the lessons of a lost decade of foreign policy, a massive body count and a huge hole in the US treasury, it stands to reason a better-informed public might prevent such future disasters. Bringing statecraft back into the light could only be an improvement, offering enormous benefits to a suddenly cash-strapped nation unable to afford more lavish adventures abroad, a nation whose haggard, stop-loss military is running on vapors.

And yet the mainstream reception of this wealth of new knowledge has been surly and resentful. The government's response to each new wave of leaks has been a syncopated alternation between shrieks of angry panic and soothing deflationary assessments of the "damage" done to US interests. (For "US interests" read: the delicate collective ego of the foreign policy elite, whose performance in the past decade has been so lethally sub-par.) A typical alternation has been Hillary Clinton's thundering denunciation of the leaked diplomatic cables as "an assault on the international community" followed by written State Department reports—confidential of course—that the national interest has not been damaged. (Manning's lawyer has already subpoenaed such reports, one by the White House, the other by Foggy Bottom.) As we have already seen, in the case of Joe Biden, sometimes it is the same official who both blasts and retracts within in the same twenty-four-hour span. (Former Secretary of Defense Robert Gates also went from accusing Wikileaks of having "blood on their hands" to a coolly dismissive assessment months later, to much less media fanfare.)

Reactions outside the government have scarcely been much different, another example of how deeply embedded America's elite media has become. On "the right," a term which also encompasses most of the Democratic Party when it comes to national security issues, the response has been simple: Kill 'em! But on the libertarian fringe of both right and left, a small but growing array of politicians, former law enforcement and security officials and journalists have defended Manning vigorously: Congressmen and presidential candidates Dr. Ron Paul (R–TX) and Dennis Kucinich (D–OH), Green Party candidate Dr. Jill Stein, Justice Party candidate and former Salt Lake City Mayor Rocky Anderson; career FBI special agent Coleen Rowley (a *Time* magazine Person of the Year in 2002) and CIA analyst Ray McGovern; columnists Jack Shafer, Glenn Greenwald and FireDogLake writers Marcy Wheeler, Jane Hamsher and Kevin Gosztola; activist David Swanson and the Bradley Manning Support Network itself. In the hegemonic center of the American media, moderately liberal on gays, guns and God but rightwing on everything else, the reception of the leaks has closely followed the government's script.

A vivid example is the sudden outpouring of concern among military and media for Afghan civilians upon the release of the Afghan War Logs. Because Wikileaks did not redact the names of all of the local informants and collaborators working with ISAF forces, it was alleged that every named Afghan was at imminent risk of a Taliban assassination. (The Taliban obliged by making such a threat.) The threat to American soldiers was also played up.

What to make of this sudden geyser of concern? Media coverage of the Af-Pak War has entailed a near denial of other civilian casualties, with even the comparatively humanist *New York Times* routinely "forgetting" to write up the Af-Pak civilian casualties to drone strikes. Even the deaths of American forces are weirdly downplayed. (August 2011 was the deadliest month yet for American forces in Afghanistan, a milestone that went virtually unremarked.)

Whether or not this newfound concern is genuine, the Department of Defense confessed to a McClatchy reporter in December 2010 that there was no evidence of a single Afghan informant being harmed in a reprisal, an assertion the DoD spokesperson echoed at a press conference days later.[46] But why dwell on the vulgar certainty of real casualties when you can keen and wail for the civilian deaths that might be caused someday, hypothetically, by Wikileaks?

This is only the first case of the government hypochondriacally groaning about the damage done by Manning's alleged leaks. Another fine example is the State Department's confidential list of vital strategic interests, the public release of which, we were warned, was soon going to trigger a Tom Clancy-style apocalypse. Pundits made a meal of this "terrorist to-do list," more proof that Julian Assange and Bradley Manning were nihilists bent on global mayhem. Brian Lehrer and George Packer, two liberal New Yorkers, clucked and scolded on Lehrer's radio show at the anti-American recklessness of Wikileaks' rash deed.[47] Of course the dreadful list turns out to be a damp squib of a let-down—informing us not only that the Congo is rich in mineral wealth, but that the Strait of Gibraltar is—get the smelling salts—a vital shipping lane.[48] The rest of the document, apparently tabulated by a reasonably capable undergraduate intern, is of a similar Wikipedia banality. Have we in America become so infantilized that tidbits of basic geography must now be state secrets? Maybe better to leave that question unanswered.

The greatest Michael Bay-produced *ragnarok* was supposed to come when Wikileaks released the whole cache of its State Department cables on September 1, 2011. (Due to a security glitch for which Julian Assange, a disgruntled former comrade and *Guardian* journalist David Leigh are responsible, the entire load of 250,000 "Cablegate" documents had become available in a far corner of the web, so Wikileaks decided to go ahead and advertise their full availability.) Suddenly all 250,000 documents were available, and in unredacted form! The State Department promised that hundreds of native informants—advocates, other diplomats, even human rights workers—would be at risk of imminent persecution. "Irresponsible, reckless and frankly dangerous," said Foggy Bottom's head flack. Once again, pundits clicked their tongues and waxed wroth—though not with quite the same gusto as before.

By now some in the media had wearied of the monotonous two-step and were looking askance at the predictions of diplomatic meltdown and savage reprisal. Some enterprising reporters with Associated Press tracked down several of the informants named in the cables to solicit their opinion. Federica Ferrari Bravo had met with US diplomats in Italy seven years before; a source so sensitive that US officials were instructed not to utter her name. According to the AP, she was baffled to learn that her identity was secret at all. "I don't think I said anything that would put me at risk," the Italian diplomat confessed. Former Malaysian diplomat Shazryl Eskay Abdullah was astonished that an "unofficial lunch meeting" years ago with a US official had been reported at all, but didn't think it mattered.[49] The *Christian Science Monitor*'s Beijing correspondent similarly found that none of the Chinese citizens named in the cables had suffered any reprisals.[50]

Not a single death has been traced to Pfc. Manning's (alleged) leaks. Yes, the identity of an Australian secret agent was revealed, at no peril to his person. Yes, two American ambassadors, to Ecuador and to Mexico, were recalled after impolitic statements were made public. (Then again, America's relationship with these two nations has become rocky as the region's self-confidence grows.) The real diplomatic shakeup has been, on the surface, quite minor—a small price to pay for this treasury of knowledge.

An Anglican minister in Baghdad bemoaned the leak of a State Department cable about the handful of remaining Jews in Baghdad. By bringing attention to this nearly vanished subculture, doesn't Wikileaks know they will hasten their persecution?[51] It was quickly pointed out by one foreign service officer on his personal blog that the prelate decrying the publicity had been a very eager source for a *Time* magazine article on the same subject not three years before.[52] We have not heard since of the horrible damage done by the Cablegate release.

Throughout the disclosures, American journalists have eagerly projected all manner of strange motives both to Wikileaks and to Pfc. Manning. (We have already seen how the private's alleged deeds have been chalked up to sexual reasons, personal reasons, emotional reasons, everything but the actual political reasons he clearly lays out to his baffled interlocutor in the incriminating chatlogs.)

It is often asserted by both government and their preferred media, without evidence, that Wikileaks is "anti-American." Even Dana Priest and William Arkin, authors of the excellent *Top Secret America*, succumb to this received idea and casually impugn Wikileaks' motives. To be sure, the group's choice to transcribe the (admittedly blood-curdling) banter of the Apache gunships in redneck phrasing complete with dropped consonants was gratuitous, and detracted from the video's effect. But then this hauteur is shared by most US intellectuals as well—hardly a sign of hating the USA. If it is "anti-American" to see the invasion of Iraq as a disaster and view the ongoing adventure in Afghanistan in a negative light, then a solid majority of the United States must also be suffering from anti-Americanism. The charge of "anti-Americanism" is less an accurate description of Wikileaks than another worrisome sign of surging xenophobia in the United States which, over ten years after 9/11, has not yet crested.

Another imputation to Wikileaks is that the endeavor is "utopian," which for America's mainstream punditry is the ultimate put-down. This mudslinging also fails to stick. Although the goal of "total transparency" has been carelessly attributed to Assange and Wikileaks by *The New Yorker* and other publications, one looks in vain through the group's published statements for utopian demands of "total transparency" or anything like it. In a nation where the government generates some 92 million classified documents a year, and where government secrecy and distortion played no small part in a disastrous war that has not quite ended, one might more accurately describe the Wikileaks endeavor as a fundamentally defensive and pragmatic effort to bring essential matters of government into the light. Instead, American pundits have worried ominously about the threat of too much transparency—a bit like worrying that the restoration of Reagan-era income tax rates might lead to gulag communism.

Bradley Manning has been very clear about the principles behind his alleged disclosure: it's important that the public should know what its government is doing. Because the Wikileaks team has said more about their own motives, they have not quite been as consistent. One thing is clear: their goals are, for better or worse, not radical, utopian or even "left wing" in the conventional sense of the term. The Wikileaks mission statement quotes Jefferson and US Supreme Court decisions, while Assange's buzzword of "populist intelligence" fits squarely within classical republican political theory. Compared to the more genuinely radical groups that exploded throughout the 1970s, Wikileaks is quite blandly establishmentarian: they want more governmental opennenss, not class struggle or revolutionary violence. They are, essentially, eighteenth-century liberals who are good with computers.

Outside the United States, the reaction to Wikileaks has been quite different—less alarmist, less panicked, less surly. Not just left or libertarian intellectuals but even heads of state and Establishment diplomats have praised both Wikileaks and Manning. Luiz Inazio "Lula" da Silva praised the anti-secrecy organization and mocked the official panic surrounding its leaks. In November, 2011, 54 center-left members of the European Parliament signed a letter condemning the treatment of Bradley Manning—but only vaguely supportive of the private's alleged disclosures. Dick Marty, a conservative Swiss politician and former prosecutor who serves as a rapporteur for the Council of Europe is much bolder in his praise of Manning in his investigation into Europe's enabling role in the CIA's "special rendition" program.[53] In the report, Marty not only condemns the growing "cult of secrecy," he demands greater public scrutiny of Europe's security services, and singles out Pfc. Bradley Manning for praise as a whistleblower, acknowledging Wikileaks' role in exposing the rendition program. Will Julian Assange soon join Pfc. Manning as a victim of these barely supervised security services?

The case of Pfc. Manning is of course hardly the first time a messenger has been shot, a whistleblower scapegoated, a light-bringer demonized. What impact do leaks really have? Knowledge is power, so the saying goes, but ignorance turns out have its own special force as well, and a public's incuriosity can be as strong as its will-to-knowledge. The value of any fact is only that which the public is willing to give it: information does nothing on its own. Have leaks ever really ended wars or brought down governments? What will the real consequences of Bradley Manning's alleged leaks be? In the next chapter we turn to the tangled and tragic relations between whistleblowers and their public.

4

WHISTLEBLOWERS AND THEIR PUBLIC

03:24:10 PM) **bradass87:** we're human... and we're killing ourselves... and no-one seems to see that... and it bothers me

(03:24:26 PM) **bradass87:** apathy

(03:25:28 PM) **bradass87:** apathy is far worse than the active participation

(05:54:42 PM) **bradass87:** apathy is its own 3rd dimension... i have special graph for that... =P

Pfc. Bradley Manning's alleged leaks have fueled thousands of stories in the world's major newspapers; they have stripped the spin and lies off the official versions of the Afghanistan War and the Iraq War; they have shined a light into the pseudo-legal prison camp of Guantánamo. The leaked diplomatic cables have provided a partial view of how the world's greatest power conducts its affairs, and candid accounts of how many nations run themselves.

What impact have these leaks had? Have they rolled back the invasion of Iraq or the occupation of Afghanistan? Have they led to the "worldwide discussion, debates, reforms" that Bradley Manning hoped for? Have they changed foreign policy? What role, for that matter, do leaks of death squads and free-fire zones ever play in ending wars and shaping statecraft?

Though the Wikileaks revelations are the largest such revelations yet, this is far from the first time state secrets have come to light. Leaks have done much to advance knowledge throughout history. The chapter on taxation in Adam Smith's *Wealth of Nations* relies entirely on a survey of European fiscal practices that the French crown intended for elite administrative use only. Roger Casement's exposés of King Leopold's Congo, of the British-owned rubber plantations of the Amazon, made him a Victorian hero—until his gunrunning for Irish independence got him hanged. Rupert Murdoch's grandfather made his name and began his press empire by leaking the Gallipoli cables. The exposure of the My Lai massacre came after a see-no-evil military investigation found nothing. (The whitewash, by the way, was led by a young Army major named Colin Powell.[1])

Many leaks, even of top-secret skullduggery, even of atrocity, have made only the slightest dent in whatever vast imperial project they were meant to expose. Even when the My Lai massacre came to light—over 500 Vietnamese villagers, including women, children, the elderly, methodically slaughtered by American troops—thanks to former helicopter door-gunner Ron Ridenhour and reporter Sy Hersh, failed utterly to halt the war, which lasted another seven years. It didn't even hold the US soldiers to account, with the commanding officer suffering only three-and-a-half years of house arrest.

It turns out the impact of whistleblowing is often minimal. When Iranian students stormed the US embassy in 1979, they seized reams of secret files related to the CIA's activities throughout the whole Middle East. After laboriously pasting together many shredded pages and translating the lot into Farsi, they began to release the multivolume edition of *Documents from the US Espionage Den*.[2] Here at last were top-secret accounts of back room American fiddling with the internal affairs and foreign ministries of the entire Middle East region, not to mention CIA involvement in enormous petroleum deals and projects.

After the mandatory panic and utterances about this grave blow to American national security from which the world would never recover, the world yawned and Washington continued its business in the Middle East, without Iran in its pocket but otherwise unchastened. In the past thirty years, the Carter Doctrine—that the Persian Gulf is of vital strategic interest to the United States and must, like the Caribbean, remain under American military control—has only grown more aggressive, while American meddling in the Middle East has intensified. Plainly, the Iranian students' game-changing revelations barely rattled Washington's imperial designs in the region.

What of the Pentagon Papers? Given their talismanic place in the folklore of the peace movement, surely this superleak dealt a deathblow against America's warmaking in Southeast Asia? The virtue of exposing the Pentagon Papers can hardly be doubted: the Department of Defense's in-house history of the Vietnam War conclusively gave the lie to upbeat official statements about that long and thoroughly gratuitous war. But the story of this mega-leak's real impact on the war—and on the press, and on the law, and on society in general—is anything but straightforward.

When the Pentagon Papers first began their appearance in the *New York Times*, President Nixon was delighted. As the papers only covered events under the previous two administrations, here was a chance to make Jack Kennedy look bad—what could be better for Dick Nixon? It was only after Henry Kissinger persuaded his boss that tolerating the leaks made him look like a weakling that Nixon's bumbling staff cocked their blunderbuss at the *Times*, and it blew up in their face.[3] The Supreme Court of the United States held, in an ambiguous ruling whose holding is still debated, that the government could not bar the *Times* from publishing these top-secret leaks. Nixon's Solicitor General who had argued the government's case later repudiated the whole effort to ban the Papers' publication. Point, press.

Next the government took woozy aim at Ellsberg, reviving the Espionage Act of 1917 with the then-novel use of punishing a domestic leaker. Nixon's stooges broke into Ellsberg's psychiatrist's office hoping to find dirt on the man. (Ellsberg, a model Marine who had graduated first in his class at Quantico's officer training school, deferred grad school at Harvard to stay on active duty, and had come under enemy fire in Vietnam, was not an easy guy to smear.) The burglars famously didn't find anything, but they eventually got caught. Once the Ellsberg trial had begun, Team Nixon attempted to bribe the judge, offering him the directorship of the Federal Bureau of Investigation—should he be interested. The judge, in his clueless vanity, only realized weeks later that he was being suborned. He hastily declared a mistrial with prejudice, leaving Ellsberg, who had always admitted to leaking the top-secret documents, a free man. Let it not be forgotten that the only legal difference between Daniel Ellsberg's confessed leak and Manning's alleged deed is that the Pentagon Papers were uniformly designated "top secret," a higher classification than anything from the WikiLeaks disclosures. Ellsberg was never acquitted.

A great story, but in the end, the Pentagon Papers did nothing to halt or even slow the Vietnam War. A paperback edition of highlights from the papers sold over a million, but few actually read it.[4] The mess did, however, hasten Nixon's self-immolation.

The litany is long of colossal game-changing bombshells that made inaudible thuds on impact. During France's vicious post-colonial war in Algeria, Henri Alleg's famous 1958 exposé of his torture by colonial authorities sold 60,000 copies in a single day. Other such testimonies were plentiful. But as Alexander Cockburn points out, "torture duly became more pervasive, and the war more savage, under the supervision of a nominally socialist French government."[5]

Much more recently, the anonymous leak of US Ambassador to Afghanistan Karl Eikenberry's cable to the White House argued forcefully and expertly (the now ex-ambassador is a retired Army general) against troop escalation and for the scrapping of the DoD's counterinsurgency strategy. The document was leaked in November 2009 and published in the *New York Times* two months later.[6] Despite Eikenberry's impeccable credentials, and despite swiftly tanking public support for the war, the cable halted neither Obama's Afghan surge nor the intensified drone strikes. And 2009–11 have been the bloodiest three years yet for American forces in Afghanistan.

We might ask—in our despair—why we ever think, like Bradley Manning, that new information will spur "worldwide debates, discussions and reforms"? Of course, secret information can result in a happy ending, and it often does—at the movies. Some critical bit of intelligence is a common Maguffin in suspense movies and pulp thrillers. Villains have suppressed some important piece of knowledge and this is causing grave harm; the protagonist after many struggles retrieves the intelligence, brings it to light, and the system rights itself in the nick of time, often thanks to the press. This plot is pure escapist fantasy, and a conservative one at that as it reaffirms faith in the normal political system and its institutions, whose essential goodness always wins out over some "abuse" or "rogue element."

It's easy to see why this plot line is so popular with screenwriters, journalists, and intellectuals generally. Intellectuals have so much invested in the power of information and knowledge, and we almost always overstate the importance of it as an engine-driver of history or motivator of human actions. The just-add-knowledge-and-stir model of political action was favored by liberals of the Enlightenment and the liberals of today, from the Encyclopedists and James Madison to Bertrand Russell and Pfc. Bradley Manning. But isn't this faith misplaced?

In his confessional chatlogs, Manning delivers his credo: "I want people to see the truth... regardless of who they are... because without information, you cannot make informed decisions as a public." But who actually wants to see the truth? Who really wants knowledge? It turns out that ignorance is not just a matter of information supply, but of demand. Ignorance is much more than an absence of knowledge, a pristine vacancy suitable for structures of knowledge to be built through "education." In fact, ignorance is more often than not something rock-solid, opaque and willful.

It can't be stressed enough that willful ignorance is not the exclusive province of working-class people or of those without formal schooling. From 2000–2008 this sort of blockheadedness found its personification in the President of the United States, a scion of multigenerational privilege.

We might then pessimistically think that the joke is on the whistleblowers, the Enlightenment true believers, all those naïve types who would "speak truth to power." Of what use has the truth ever been in politics? When Secretary of State Colin Powell testified at the General Assembly that he had incontrovertible proof of Iraq's weapons of mass destruction, his whole dishonorable speech collapsed around him only hours later, when key assertions were revealed as a shoddy internet cut-and-paste job, giving the whole *casus belli* a nightmarish *Alice in Wonderland* quality.[7] Of course the quick and definitive unmasking of official lies did nothing to halt the war juggernaut: the government, the major media, and ultimately millions of Americans had too much invested in war—politically, financially, psychologically—to reverse course.

The consequences of knowledge can be nil; they can also be perverse. The dangerous knowledge brought to light by social reformers often has unexpected consequences. The upshot of Upton Sinclair's exposé of hazardous working conditions in the meatpacking industry wasn't worker safety laws, but sanitary measures designed to protect middle-class consumers. The results of Jacob Riis' muckraking photographs of working-class New Yorkers was punitive legislation to better "motivate" the slum-dwellers, like shuttering the police precinct bunkhouses that had served as informal homeless shelters. Governments and their embedded media outlets have managed to spin some of the Wikileaks revelations in directions that astonish. Even as every world newspaper seized on the Guantánamo files to show the incompetent harshness of the prison camp—including the quite conservative British *Daily Telegraph*—the *New York Times* emphasized just how dangerous the inmates were—even though nearly three out of four have been released.

"What does end wars?" asks Alexander Cockburn. "One side is annihilated, the money runs out, the troops mutiny, the government falls, or fears it will. With the US war in Afghanistan none of these conditions has yet been met."

Despair over truth's impotence is not fully warranted. Information may not be sufficient, but it is necessary, and when harnessed to political will, it can change the world. After all, Daniel Ellsberg's earlier, though far less famous, 1968 leak of a top-secret report to the president may well have forestalled a catastrophic widening of the war, at least until Nixon and Kissinger carpet-bombed Cambodia. Therein, chairman of the Joint Chiefs of Staff General Earle Wheeler requested an additional 206,000 US troops for Vietnam, which would have entailed calling up the reserves and widening the war into Laos, Cambodia; the report also contemplated the use of "small tactical" nuclear weapons not just in North Vietnam but in the south as well. Ellsberg handed the document to Robert F. Kennedy, who rallied Senate opposition to the escalation; someone else had passed the plans to the *New York Times*.[8] President Johnson did not request the troop increase.

Were American air strikes on Iran in the waning days of Bush-Cheney averted by a timely leak? The 2007 National Intelligence Estimate on Iran's nuclear program swiftly made its way public; its findings—that Iran was very far from acquiring nuclear weapons—were a shocking reversal of previous reports. Admiral William Fallon, head of CENTCOM, took the unusual step of immediately declassifying this NIE on Iran in December, 2007; a decision to which the White House, fearing an inevitable leak, assented. This quasi-leak, whose content was given emphatic backing by top military, diplomatic and intelligence officials, further stated that "We judge with high confidence that in fall 2003, Tehran halted its nuclear weapons program." This was Fallon making good on his candid earlier utterance that "we won't be doing Iran on my watch"—candor that cost him his job.[9]

In his memoirs, George W. Bush writes that this unexpected assessment "tied my hands on the military side."[10] It's impossible to prove that this quasi-leak was decisive in preventing American and/or Israeli air strikes (or worse) on Iran. But it certainly did set back the neoconservative efforts to make war on Tehran, with much disappointment manifested in the National Review and editorial section of the Wall Street Journal.

It was Ray McGovern, a retired CIA senior analyst, who brought the above two leaks to my attention. McGovern knows something about secrets, intelligence and public service: he served in Army intelligence in

Vietnam, then went on to give daily intelligence briefings to President Reagan and the first Bush.

McGovern has written that he wished he had had the courage to leak some of the Pentagon's honest internal evaluations of the Vietnam War's countless failings and evils—back then, he tells me, the Fourth Estate actually picked up stories like that, and it could have given the antiwar movement a boost.[10] (Today McGovern works with Tell the Word, a publishing ministry of the ecumenical Church of the Savior in inner-city Washington; he's also a co-founder of Veteran Intelligence Professionals for Sanity.) On February 15, 2011, McGovern attended a speech given by Secretary of State Hillary Clinton. Eager to disassociate himself from what he called "the obsequious adulation of a person responsible for so much death, suffering and destruction," McGovern stood up in the midst of her opening remarks, and turned his back to her, his Veterans for Peace t-shirt combining with his silence to make a powerful statement. It did not go unnoticed. Madame Secretary's security retinue grabbed McGovern, dragged him out of the auditorium, beating him black and blue. "So this is America! So this is America!" he yelled. Clinton resumed her speech, a lofty defense of internet freedom—abroad, of course, not at home.[11]

Ray is an unpretentious guy from the Bronx; a self-professed "Vatican II Catholic;" a polyglot intellectual proficient in five languages. We talked about Brad Manning's alleged act—which McGovern admires greatly—its likely impact on US foreign policy, and Thomas Aquinas. "In section 158 of the *Summa Theologica*, Aquinas complains that Latin has no word for the virtue of anger. There's anger as a vice, *iracundia*. So Aquinas went back to Chrysostom to revive the concept of righteous anger at injustice and evil. Because he who isn't angry has an 'unreasoned patience', sows the seeds of vice. I'm trying to be virtuously angry. Being Irish gives you a leg up!

"Bradley Manning had the strength to be angry. Are all of the cables he released covered by whistleblower protection laws? Of course not, but what was he going to do, go over each and every one in his bed with a flashlight? Moral philosophy teaches that there are supervening values that dwarf the other stuff, that it's transcendently important to stop war and torture. That's what I think Manning understood, these basic principles.

"But in America today we have far too much passive acceptance of injustice. We need more righteous anger."[12]

McGovern's gloomy diagnosis is, alas, born out by hard data. We Americans can pride ourselves all we want on our anti-authority posturing, but a 2006 poll from the International Social Survey Programme of national attitudes towards individualism and authority tells a very different story.

In 2006, the ISSP asked the question "In general, would you say that people should obey the law without exception, or are there exceptional occasions on which people should follow their consciences even if it means breaking the law?" At 45 percent, Americans were the least likely out of nine nationalities to say that people should at least on occasion follow their consciences—far fewer than, for example, the Swedes (70 percent) and the French (78 percent). Similarly, in 2003, Americans turned out to be the most likely to embrace the statement "People should support their country even if the country is in the wrong."[13]

Perhaps the most distressing part of the whole saga of these leaks is that, given how easy it was to bring these public records to light, and how many soldiers and diplomats had access to them, not a single person had the courage to do the deed—until, allegedly, a certain private from Crescent, Oklahoma. This paucity of public-spirited citizens speaks poorly of American rebelliousness. After all, what country can remain free if its citizens no longer have any "issues with authority"?

If any lesson can be drawn from the Manning affair, it's that leaks can make a great difference if there is organized political muscle to put them to good use. Information on its own is futile; as useless as those other false hopes of the global center-left, international law and its sidekick, the human rights industry, all of which have their uses, but are insufficient to stop wars and end torture. This is not to denigrate the achievement of the person who gave us this magnificent gift of knowledge about world affairs. If the disclosures have not changed US statecraft—yet—the fault lies not in the cables, but in the pathetic lack of political organization among those individuals who don't "have a position" in Halliburton stock—the 99%, if you will.

Michael Moore has named Bradley Manning a patron saint of the Occupy Wall Street phenomenon, an icon and martyr for the cause of justice and freedom. The "Free Bradley" signs at Occupy events all over the country are often sneered at as proof of the incipient movement's indiscipline and lack of realism. They are, in fact, a sign of the group's robust ideals and healthy distance from the neoliberal/neoconservative mainstream of American news media.

For now, the disclosures and their great potential hangs unresolved. Will the leaks kindle more uprisings in authoritarian nations? Will the Haitian diaspora be able to use the diplomatic cables to rally opposition to imperial meddling? Will Americans unlearn some of their deference and docility and stand up to the foreign policy elite that has brought carnage and destruction to Iraq, Afghanistan, Pakistan, that has supported dictators in Egypt, Yemen, Bahrain and bankrolled ethnic cleansing in Palestine? Will American stand against a foreign policy that has served their own needs and interests so disastrously? The growing number of young returned veterans at Occupy Wall Street events is a sign that their fellow soldier and patriot's earnest hopes for debate, discussion and reform may yet be validated.

But even if these leaks lead to nothing, the Promethean act of bringing knowledge to mere civilians without a security clearance is still taboo enough to provoke the severest punishment.

5

THE TORTURE OF BRADLEY MANNING

(2:01:14 PM) **bradass87**: but im pretty desperate for some non-isolation

No feature of the Manning affair has been more controversial than the young soldier's nine months under strict solitary confinement at the Quantico Marine Corps Base. As we have seen, even the State Department's top spokesperson, a mouthpiece of perfect blandness, lost his job after a spontaneous eruption damning Manning's treatment, and foreign governments have brought pressure to bear, sending pointed letters of concern to Washington.

Adrian Lamo, shortly after informing on Manning, assured an audience of hackers and digital activists in New York that his dupe would be treated decently; after all, "We don't torture our own citizens."[1] Lamo was apparently trying to distinguish Manning's likely treatment from that endured by hundreds of captured foreigners in the course of our Global War on Terror, or GWOT, as it was known in-house during the Bush-Cheney Administration.

Lamo's reassurance, based perhaps in guilt-ridden wishfulness, has proven grotesquely wrong. Twenty-three hours of solitary a day; a ban even on push-ups and sit-ups in the cell; the confiscation even of reading glasses; enforced nudity at night; the unrelenting repetitive mental stress of having to respond every five waking minutes to the guards' query, "Are you OK?" If this were done to a US soldier held captive in North Korea or Iran, no American pundit would hesitate to call this torture. How could this treatment not drive anyone mad?

Being alone in a small cell for years or even months does a body great harm. Not surprisingly, medical research into the effects of solitary confinement finds that the treatment inflicts lasting severe damage. "Solitary confinement can have serious psychological, psychiatric and sometimes physiological effects on many prison inmates," writes Dr. Peter Scharff Smith, head of research at the Danish Institute for Human Rights. "A long list of possible symptoms from insomnia and confusion to hallucinations and outright insanity has been documented."[2] The suicide rate for isolated inmates, according to another psychiatric expert on mental health in prisons, is substantially higher than among those living communally in prison.

In the footsteps of medical science, international law is ever less hesitant to classify solitary confinement as torture. The European Court of Human Rights has allowed the practice in the case of Kurdish terrorist Abdullah Öcalan, but after finding a marked mental deterioration in that prisoner recommended that the Turkish government integrate him into a communal setting.[3] The United States has ratified the international Convention Against Torture, whose acting body, the Committee Against Torture, has recommended that long-term solitary be wholly abolished. The German Bundestag's human rights committee was not breaking new ground when it condemned Manning's treatment as torture.

But what could possibly inspire the American government to torture one of its own citizens? Most of those who have answered this question have approached the problem from the context of America's post-9/11 GWOT. Andy Worthington, the most dogged and incisive journalistic tracker of the Guantánamo prison, has asked if Bradley Manning is being treated like an enemy combatant.[4] Lisa Hajjar, a trenchant academic analyst of Washington's weaponization of international law, has described the treatment of Manning as a slide down the "slippery slope," from torturing enemy combatants to inflicting the same punishment on Americans, just as torture opponents predicted would happen.[5]

It is certainly tempting to see the isolation torture of Bradley Manning as toxic spillover from the Global War on Terror. What else could explain an advanced industrial democracy thus abusing one of its own citizens?

There is undoubtedly some truth to this story—that after a decade, the "excesses" of the War on Terror have seeped into our domestic justice systems. Yet this account is, by itself, incomplete. In fact this narrative is perhaps undeservedly reassuring. For this story assumes that our domestic criminal justice system was already uncontaminated, and had hitherto run smoothly and fairly, at least more or less. This narrative of corruption assumes that Abu Ghraib, Bagram and Guantánamo are flagrant offenses against "American values," vivid exceptions to our legal and penal norms. It assumes that nine months pretrial detention in solitary confinement is simply unheard-of in the United States. In short, this story assumes the legalized torture of Bradley Manning to be exceptional, an atrocity. We must reject these assumptions: they are wrong both in their particulars and in their overall image of America's justice system.

The roots of Abu Ghraib, Bagram, Guantánamo and the isolation torture of Bradley Manning are so close to home that we have trouble seeing them. Many of us would like to think that all of this is a colossal and shameful exception to our laws and customs. But the sensational

GWOT atrocities that have scandalized the world for the past decade are at base a simple extension of our everyday "normal" way of doing criminal justice. To be sure, the GWOT's use of torture has been more programmatic, and the locales more exotic, but on the whole these headline-making scandals have been far less aberrant than we would like to think. From Guantánamo to the treatment of Bradley Manning, most of our supposedly out-of-character response to 9/11 has in fact been less exception than the rule. On the whole, the GWOT has been all-American.

This is a strong statement, demanding evidence beyond the scope of the Bradley Manning case. The argument is best bolstered by a brief and unpleasant visit to Guantánamo, the iconic "legal black hole" whose essential *normality* within the American legal-penal galaxy is more disturbing still.

I visited Guantánamo in April–May of 2010, where a member of our international press gaggle let it slip that she didn't much care for the place. "*This*," she confided to the group, "is the *worst* place I have *ever* visited in my *entire career*." Many of us made similar judgments over the course of our visit.

It's not hard to see why so many of us felt this way: we were covering pretrial hearings for the trial of Omar Khadr, a Canadian captured at age 15 after a firefight with US forces outside Kabul in 2002, tortured and interrogated for a few months at Bagram Air Base in Afghanistan, then transported to Guantánamo to await trial before a military commission, charged with five "war crimes." (The scare-quotes are necessary as four of the charges were freshly invented for the occasion, and are not recognized as war crimes in any other court.) In October later that year, Khadr would take a deal pleading guilty to all charges, leaving him with one more year at Gitmo–to be spent in solitary–and then a likely transfer to Canada for a remaining seven years of either prison or supervised release.

Aside from Khadr and about 130 other prisoners who may one day see a trial, Guantánamo still holds some 45 more War on Terror prisoners who will be "detained" indefinitely without being tried at all. This is one of the radical policies of George W. Bush and Dick Cheney that is now cheerfully defended by the human rights grandees in Barack Obama's State Department.

Gitmo and all other places without *habeas corpus* rights are indeed dismal places—and there is certainly something striking about the first conviction of a child soldier since World War II. All the same, I couldn't help but draw a comparison from the most notorious prison in the world to homegrown US federal prisons, like the one in Terre Haute, Indiana (whose maximum security wing was copied down to the smallest detail at Gitmo's Camp 5), or even a run-of-the-mill overcrowded state penitentiary, the kind you pass on the highway without even noticing, or one of the crumbling youth detention facilities in New York State which are thoroughly hellish.

Such prisons may lack the exotic setting of Gitmo's Camp Delta, but they are not incomparable. A great many of America's domestic prisons also routinely abuse inmates; are unable or unwilling to prevent inmate rape; inflict long-term solitary confinement, which does at least as much physiological damage as waterboarding; and in actual practice operate beyond most notions of the rule of law. Confessions, true or false, obtained through violence and threats, aren't restricted to Guantánamo either. They are not all that hard to find in our fifty states. And for the rest of our prison system, where is the outraged international press gaggle? Why are no British "law lords" calling the federal supermax in Florence, Colorado, a "legal black hole" as Lord Johan Steyn termed Guantánamo?

Alas, in so many ways Guantánamo is not the exception but far closer to the rule of our criminal justice system. To be sure, taking a child soldier you've captured in a foreign land, whose interrogation entailed stringing him up half-naked in a five-foot-square cell with wrists chained to the bars at eye level and a hood clamped tightly over his face, then prosecuting him for "murder" because he allegedly tossed a grenade on a foreign battlefield, does present some legal issues that don't ordinarily come up in Spokane or Chillicothe.

But are Gitmo, the torture of Bradley Manning and the whole Global War on Terror a "betrayal of American values"? Would that they were. For nearly every grisly tabloid feature of the Khadr case, you can find an easy analog in our everyday criminal justice system. In a sense, much of our War on Terror has proven a slightly spicier version of our "normal" way of doing criminal justice. Using the case of young Omar Khadr, let's take this step by step.

Child Soldiers and Juvenile Offenders

Hasn't there been a surge of concern for child soldiers in book clubs and church groups across the land? It turns out that this long-distance compassion goes up in smoke at closer range. When a child soldier points his gun at an American, not another African, he becomes a hardened terrorist in American eyes.

The hypocrisy in all this is perhaps only apparent. After all, clemency for youth offenders, be they child soldiers or just local kids, runs against the American grain today. If we routinely prosecute children even younger than 15 as adults—and we do—why should a foreign child soldier be any different?

In fact the US even has a few dozen inmates doing life without parole for acts committed when they were thirteen or fourteen, and most of these sentences were mandatory rather than the prerogative of a particularly vindictive judge. (Some progress has been made: in May 2010, the United States Supreme Court decided in *Graham v. Florida* that juveniles can get life without parole *only* if there's homicide involved.)[6] Overall, the US has in recent years had precious little mercy for its children, or anyone else's.

During my visit to Gitmo, the press corps gasped when Khadr's "Interrogator Number One," Joshua Claus, described the veiled threats of rape he wielded at Bagram Prison to try to break the young prisoner. If Khadr should fail to cooperate, Claus told him, he would meet the same fate as another young (and imaginary) Afghan detainee who was supposedly sent to a US penitentiary and raped to death in a shower room by "neo-Nazis, and four big black guys." Claus, a court-martialed detainee abuser, had been the leader of the final interrogation of a mistakenly imprisoned Afghan taxi driver who was beaten to death by American guards at Bagram in 2002. Before receiving a light sentence in the case, Claus pledged his full cooperation with the Khadr prosecution, and he kept his part of the bargain with visible enthusiasm.

As it happens, Claus' veiled threats of rape and violence to a minor would not have been so uncommon in domestic interrogation rooms. "From the stories I'm familiar with, threats like that are a pretty garden-variety police interrogation tactic," says Locke Bowman, legal director of the MacArthur Justice Center at Northwestern University. With youths, it's not that much of a challenge to get a false confession, even without the threat of or actual physical violence being brought to bear, as the case of Marty Tankleff in Long Island shows, not to mention the seven and eight-year-old boys from the Englewood neighborhood of Chicago who, in the summer of 1998, "confessed" to murdering a girl for her bicycle. Even after DNA evidence from semen found on the corpse was matched to an adult serial sex offender, the Chicago Police Superintendent at first refused to exonerate them. The State's Attorney might well have prosecuted the boys, too, if the entire South Side of Chicago hadn't threatened to explode.[7]

Torture

We bemoan with great feeling that America has "become" a state that uses torture. Alas, this, too, is not so new, nor has it ever been limited to foreign insurgents (be they Comanche, Filipino, or Vietnamese) or suspected terrorists. Take, for example, the former high-ranking Chicago police detective Jon Burge who, over a 20-year career, enhanced his interrogations with mock executions, suffocation, electroshocks, pistol-whipping, and yes, a form of waterboarding. All this was uncovered in 2002 in an epic special investigation which led to the reexamination of more than 100 cases, several overturned convictions, multiple Governor's pardons and the usual massive lawsuits against the Chicago Police Department. Because the statute of limitations for Burge's crimes had run out, the disgraced police officer was convicted in June, 2010 of perjury and obstruction of justice.

As for routinized prison abuse, Bagram and Abu Ghraib have regularly been described as one-off aberrations, but the origins of such brutality are not hard to spot in our treatment of prisoners at home. This continuity is personified by Charles Graner, the ringleader of the Abu Ghraib torture. Prior to his deployment, he had worked as a guard at maximum-security State Correctional Institute-Greene in southwestern Pennsylvania, itself subject to a major prisoner-abuse scandal in the late 1990s which got several guards fired, though not Graner.

The fact is, the abuse and/or torture of prisoners, though far from systematic, is not all that uncommon in many American prisons. What came out in the Abu Ghraib photos is, according to the (increasingly busy) United States program of Human Rights Watch, not so different from the abuse and brutality of many of our own stateside lock-ups.

In New York, for instance, a state task force convened by Governor David Paterson in 2008 deemed the entire youth detention system "broken."[8] The official report found that guards throughout the system regularly used "excessive force" on youth inmates, sometimes breaking bones and shattering teeth. And prison abuse here at home can be just as fatal as at Bagram. In New York, an emotionally disturbed fifteen-year-old died in 2006 after corrections officers pinned him face down on the ground. (Remember, at Bagram the interrogators tried to make young Khadr talk by threatening to send him to *an American prison*, which they apparently considered at least as threatening as anything Afghanistan had to offer.)

This is not lost on lawyers representing Gitmo detainees. "I might well advise a client to take ten years in the communal wing of Guantánamo over three years in solitary at the supermax in Florence," says Shayana Kadidal, senior managing attorney at the Guantánamo Global Justice Initiative at the Center for Constitutional Rights. Attorney Joshua Dratel, who took part in the very successful defense of Gitmo detainee David Hicks, told me that he thought the worst American-run prison is not Guantánamo's Camp Delta, but rather the Metropolitan Correctional Center in lower Manhattan. And yet, somewhat mysteriously, American intellectuals are more likely to know about the brutality of Gitmo, Abu Ghraib and Bradley Manning's nine months in Quantico than the fatal abuse and abysmal prison conditions in their own state.

To be sure, in significant ways Gitmo and the CIA's various global "black sites" were significantly worse. First, the use of torture has been far more widespread at Bagram, Abu Ghraib, Guantánamo, and the other secret prisons established in the Bush years than at home. In addition, the government has also made the decision to imprison some detainees without trial for the duration of what has often been described as a "multigenerational" global war on terror. Even those prisoners with habeas rights have had trouble getting release orders granted by the judiciary enforced. Half a dozen Guantánamo prosecutors prosecutors, not defense lawyers—have quit in disgust with the whole process, offering harsh words about the structural flaws which tilt the system towards securing convictions at the expense of impartial justice. In important ways, however, our domestic justice system is no better. Darrell Vandeveld is a former Guantánamo prosecutor. He resigned in a crisis of conscience in 2009. He was also once a public defender in San Diego where he found that many defendants were able to get only a semblance of justice. "Most of the defendants' rights were honored only in the breach. It's an overburdened system that has only become worse. Comparable to Gitmo? No doubt." Vandeveld, who now heads the public defender office in Erie, Pennsylvania, stresses that, while the outrages are not identical, they are comparable.[9]

Gazing into Gitmo's legal abyss can also easily provoke disturbing reflections on the rule of law in wartime America. As another lawyer remarked 2,000 years ago while his republic was degenerating into empire, "*Inter armas silent leges.*" (In time of war, the laws fall silent).

Keep in mind that the Global War on Terror—a term the Obama administration has demurely discarded without dropping the war so signified—is by no means the only war deforming our justice system. For the past three decades, the War on Crime and the War on Drugs have been in full fury, becoming ever less metaphorical as budgets for police and prisons skyrocket, and then skyrocket some more. These domestic crackdowns have come with much martial rhetoric and political manipulation of fear and anger, clearing a wide path for the excesses of that Global War on Terror. By overburdening the criminal courts and prison system to a hitherto unimaginable degree, these "wars" also created legal black holes where the rule of law is notional at best.

Take the Prison Litigation Reform Act of 1995, which made it nearly impossible for inmates to sue prison authorities, and has put thousands of Americans beyond the reach of any kind of judicial authority. According to Bryan Stevenson, a peerless capital-defense litigator and executive director of the Equal Justice Initiative in Montgomery, Alabama:

> US prison officials have obtained greater and greater discretion to send someone to solitary confinement for years; to force people into their cells naked, without meals; to inflict punitive measures without any possibility of outside intervention. It's often a closed system whose managers have all the authority, especially at our supermax facilities. They function in many ways like Guantánamo.[10]

Gitmo, Bagram and the solitary cell at Quantico were well within our capabilities before 9/11. Bush Administration officials and pundits told us with excitement about how, in our counterattack on al-Qaeda, "the gloves were coming off." For a great many Americans, however, those gloves had never been on to begin with. This raises some vexing questions about how we budget our indignation. Violent interrogations, abuse, and torture somehow become more scandalous when they happen overseas than in Chicago. It was just this indignation gap between abuses abroad and at home that inspired two veteran journalists, Jean Casella and James Ridgway, to found the advocacy group Solitary Watch. As they have tirelessly and eloquently pointed out, it is not clear why outrage over long-term solitary should be confined to the case of a twenty-four-year-old whistleblower named Bradley Manning, given that he was not alone in suffering legalized torture.

Manning's controversial isolation opened the eyes of many both to the horrors of solitary confinement—and to just how *uncontroversial* its pervasive use has become in the United States. For isolation is hardly some rare form of extreme punishment reserved for alleged national security threats: in the United States, its use is frequent and widespread. Manning's isolation cell at Quantico Marine Base was anything but an anomaly. It was an invisibly normal feature of the American landscape, just like baseball diamonds and strip malls.

Long-term solitary confinement is a routine component of the American penal system. The numbers speak for themselves: today there are more than 20,000 inmates in America's "supermax" prisons, which by definition keep their wards in long-term isolation. There are perhaps 50,000 to 80,000 more held in solitary in other federal and local prisons— how many exactly is not known. No one is counting.

Can torture really be so widespread in a wealthy democracy during a florescence of human rights law? Yes. As Solitary Watch notes, over the past thirty years prisoners held in solitary have shot up even faster than the US's already skyrocketing incarceration rate. Some prisoners, of course, have been put into solitary because they are a danger to other inmates and to prison guards. But a great many are now put into solitary as a disciplinary measure of the very first resort. California is especially profligate with throwing prisoners into isolation: as of July 2011, all but twenty-six of 1,056 inmates held in isolation at Pelican Bay prison were held not because of any specific infraction or violation but because of suspected gang membership. According to the Los Angeles *Times*, "[n] early 300 had been there for more than a decade, seventy-eight for more than twenty years."[11]

What, then, distinguishes Bradley Manning from the tens of thousands of Americans who are still doing long-term solitary? Is it the political nature of the charges? This argument is unsupported, for there are dozens of animal rights activists, radical environmentalists and Islamic militants isolated in "Communication Management Units" at the supermax prisons in Terre Haute and Marion, Illinois. And yet they have not received media attention or letters of concern from the Bundestag.

Of course, Manning's nine months of solitary were pretrial detention—surely that must be an aberration, to isolate any accused person for so long before any determination of guilt or innocence? This too is wishful thinking; pretrial detention in solitary is not at all uncommon in the United States. According to Casella and Ridgeway, we who are shocked by Manning's treatment

> need to be introduced to the fifteen-year-old boy who, along with several dozen other juveniles, is in isolation in a jail in Harris County, Texas, while he awaits trial on a robbery charge. He is one of hundreds—if not thousands—of prisoners being held in pretrial solitary confinement, for one reason or another, on any given day in America. Most of them lack decent legal representation, or are simply too poor to make bail.[12]

Long-term solitary confinement, even of pretrial suspects, is just one of the things the American government does, like paving roads and delivering the mail.

How can this be legal in America? Doesn't the Eighth Amendment proscribe "cruel and unusual" punishment? Those are the words, but the Supreme Court of the United States has decided that solitary confinement, even long-term isolation, does not meet that standard of cruelty and unusualness, provided that the prisoner didn't already suffer from mental illness. (That the punishment inflicts long-term psychiatric damage did not concern a majority of the judges.) Similarly, the Fourteenth Amendment's guarantee of due process under the law also does not, as presently interpreted, bar the penalty.

It should be noted that the growing outrage against Manning's treatment reflects longstanding humanitarian principles. In the nineteenth century, critics of long-term isolation were numerous and uncompromising. Charles Dickens was appalled by the practice as he observed it on a visit to America; conservative thinker Alexis de Tocqueville himself noted that the solitary confinement in Auburn, New York

> proved fatal for the majority of prisoners. It devours the victim incessantly and unmercifully; it does not reform, it kills. The unfortunate creatures submitted to this experiment wasted away.[13]

Many states of the union experimented with penal isolation before abandoning the practice in the late nineteenth century: the effects were just too devastating on inmates. Even the Supreme Court of the United States came within a whisker of abolishing long-term isolation in the 1890 case of *In re Medley*.[14]

Bradley Manning's treatment may have been atypical in the Quantico Marine Corps Base brig, and needless to say, the factual allegations in this case are unique. But then, the circumstances and the suffering of the tens of thousands of other prisoners doing long-term solitary are all unique. The cruel reality is that Pfc. Manning's nine months of isolation torture was not even remotely exceptional. What is surprising is that we in America were surprised by it at all.

It is no coincidence that many of the public figures who have pointed out the essential congruence of the Global War on Terror with US domestic criminal justice—journalists like Margaret Kimberley and Bob Herbert, and law professor James Forman, Jr.—are African-American.[15] Black Americans, whose overall incarceration rate today is probably higher than that of Soviet citizens at the peak of the gulag, have long had ample reasons over the centuries, and now as much as ever, to doubt the fundamental rightness of the American justice system.

Both the international outcry over Bradley Manning's torture and the comparative silence over the tens of thousands of other Americans enduring similar treatment have not escaped comment from the black engagé intelligentsia. Jared Ball of Morgan State University argues that the outrage over Manning's treatment is fully warranted—but not the shock, given that such treatment is so widespread already.[16] And the dissent over Manning's treatment, combined with near silence over the thousands of other Americans undergoing the very same treatment, evinces a certain moral myopia. However much we would like, we cannot pretend that the torture of Bradley Manning in solitary confinement is a blemish on an otherwise pristine justice system.

It is past time to connect the GWOT's programmatic use of torture, including solitary confinement, with the widespread application of similar treatment at home. In fact it's worth asking why these dots haven't been connected all along. Is it because so many of our domestic inmates, especially in the regions where elite national opinion is produced, are African-American and Latino, whereas most of our professional social reformers in the nonprofit sector are white and Asian-American? Is it because most of our elite public-interest lawyers and white-shoe *pro bono* advocates come out of a top half-dozen law schools where they most likely got a nice taste of well-tended federal courts, but little if any exposure to our overburdened state criminal courts? Is it just too depressing to think about our collapsing, overstrained criminal justice system in Guantánamo-like terms? Whatever the reasons, the gaping legal voids in our domestic justice and penal system have acquired the seamless invisibility of an open secret.

In fact, it's the grinding *familiarity* of much of the War on Terror's nastiness, with the draconian confinement of Bradley Manning very much included, that may best explain why many Americans view such horrors with a weary shrug. A common response to the high-minded shock-horror is exasperation tinged with resentment. *Hello, this has been going on right here at home for decades. Where the hell have you been?*

Even in the postwar twentieth century, solitary confinement was not always a natural feature of the American penal system. Other paths were possible, and still are. Just as the construction boom in supermax prisons swept the United States, Great Britain took an opposite approach to dealing with troublesome inmates, finding controlled ways to increase prisoner sociability, autonomy and responsibility with the result of significantly reduced prison violence.[17] That this solution may strike us as counterintuitive is a sign of how far we have traveled in just a few decades from the very notion of prisoner rehabilitation.

In the United States, alternatives to mass solitary confinement are not only possible, they are flourishing. Despite the Clinton years' huge construction boom in supermax prisons, solitary confinement is not a habit that is impossible to kick. Compelled by an ACLU lawsuit, Mississippi emptied out the 1000-bed supermax isolation wing of Parchman, the notorious Unit 32, famous for its howls, flooding toilets, stifling heat and chronic violence (and, in its pre-supermax days, for being the destination of incarcerated Freedom Riders during the civil rights struggles of 1961).[18] The move was justified not on humanitarian grounds but as a cost-saving measure, as it surely was.

The American media and intellectual class is slowly noticing the normalized crisis of mass solitary confinement. The New York Bar Association has recently issued a condemnation of long-term isolation. The *New Yorker* spotlighted the issue in a widely read article by a physician on the deep damage done by the punishment.[19] (As for the prospect of international law influencing national discourse, this is a red herring: international law wields very little influence or authority in the United States.)

Most important are the efforts of American prisoners themselves to roll back the practice of solitary confinement. In July 2011, the 1,056 inmates at Pelican Bay's supermax wing launched a hunger strike that spread throughout the California state prison system, even to its outsourced facilities in other states, involving 6,600 prisoners at its peak.[20] The prisoners forced an admission from the California Department of Corrections and Rehabilitation that there was "some validity to what the inmates' concerns were"—but the other modest concessions—warm hats, wall calendars, and a promise to reconsider the isolation regs—have not been implemented. The Pelican Bay hunger strike will surely not be the last organized mass uprising of American prisoners whom the state is inexorably driving insane. "We're taking prisoners who were marginally neurotic and evolving them into people who are truly psychotic," says Peter Schey, president of the Los Angeles-based Center for Human Rights and Constitutional Law. "And then we let them out."[21] In September 2011, the Pelican Bay hunger strikes began again, with 4,200 inmates across eight California prisons refusing meals.[22]

The punitive confinement of Bradley Manning, far from being an anomaly, has been consistent with American laws and customs. Why should this obvious truth be so difficult to admit? Andrew Napolitano, the former judge and steadfastly libertarian television personality, denounced the Obama Administration's treatment of Manning as "KGB tactics," and one can hardly disagree. But the epithet, connoting a radically un-American *foreignness*, is surely misplaced. The torture of Bradley Manning has been wholly in the American grain.

6

THE RULE OF LAW AND BRADLEY MANNING

(02:27:47 PM) bradass87: i mean, we're better in some respects... we're much more subtle... use a lot more words and legal techniques to legitimize everything

(02:28:00 PM) bradass87: its better than disappearing in the middle of the night

(02:28:19 PM) bradass87: but just because something is more subtle, doesn't make it right

Rules are rules. Pundits, lay and professional, aghast at Bradley Manning's alleged lawbreaking have emphasized the point. Extreme over-classification is a problem, and Manning might have (allegedly) uncovered some bad stuff, but violating the oath to protect government secrets warrants the severest consequences because... rules are rules. Never mind that the only oath a soldier takes is to uphold the Constitution; never mind that the national defense of the United States and extreme over-classification are antithetical. All this is irrelevant, because the highest truth for many Americans seems to be that *rules are rules*.

Like all tautologies, the identity "Rules = Rules" ought to be airtight, foolproof, axiomatically sealed. But beware: tautologies are usually the last panicked redoubt of authority in peril; they carry a whiff of desperation. And what the whole Manning affair teaches us is that in early twenty-first-century America, rules are very frequently ignored. If a rule is only selectively enforced it ceases to be a rule and becomes something else—an arbitrary instrument of authority, a weapon of the powerful—but not a rule. The law's draconian enforcement against Bradley Manning, set alongside the law's lackadaisical nonenforcement against the American power elite, highlights a worrisome trend: the erosion of equality before the law.

The rules-are-rules condemnation of Manning's alleged leaks has been widespread, from anonymous website commentators to the President of the United States. This is not surprising: given that the harm done by the leaks is only speculated and theorized rather than actually proven and documented, this angle of attack is perhaps all that's available to Wikileaks' enemies. Barack Obama, who campaigned as the whistleblower's friend, has responded to the Manning affair with schoolmasterly lecturing. "He broke the law," the Commander-in-Chief said to the group of Manning supporters who disrupted a Democratic Party fundraiser in San Francisco. Obama told them that the same law applies to the President and private alike:

> I have to abide by certain rules of classified information. If I were to release materials I weren't allowed to, I'd be breaking the law. We're a nation of laws. We don't let individuals make their own decision about how the laws operate.

This is a textbook description of the Rule of Law—in John Adams' words, we are "a nation of laws, not men." But is this how our system really works?

In fact, as we have already seen, elite leaks of classified material to the media are frequent and routine—an accepted means for official Washington to communicate with the public. There is no legal distinction between the leak of, say, the classified drone strike procedures by some unnamed CIA official and what Bradley Manning allegedly did. High government officials frequently break the law with impunity, recognizing—correctly—that informing the public of nearly all matters of foreign policy is no threat to national security. And no matter what such officials say to Bob Woodward or Seymour Hersh, they are prosecuted only in the rarest circumstances. Our law-professor-in-chief may lecture otherwise, but when official Washington decides to leak, the law fades away.

On the other hand, when the same laws are applied to an Army private, they take on the force of a thunderbolt. Are rules still rules? Increasingly, perhaps especially since the autumn of 2001, many of our most important rules—those related to war and the diverse set of practices known as "national security"—have turned out to be merely sets of words strung together, of no great consequence.

Were the rules really rules when the United States launched its war against Iraq in the spring of 2003? The United Nations charter, which proscribes aggressive wars, a category that very much includes preventive wars, was as gleefully flouted as if it were an archaic town ordinance prohibiting jump-rope on the Sabbath. The result has been a bloodbath, costly in human life and money. (To repeat the appalling stat that is this book's mournful bass line, the American military response to 9/11 has killed at the very least 140,000 civilians, 8,300 American soldiers and military contractors and cost the US some $3.7 trillion.) Nevertheless, calls that the Bush-Cheney leadership be held accountable for this destructive act of aggression have been brushed aside, as have demands that the torture regime and mass illegal wiretapping also be investigated and punished.

Today, as chaos rules Iraq, the elite officials who launched the war face no consequences. Bush and Cheney, Rumsfeld and Rice and several more have published bestselling memoirs, self-exonerations blaming the cataclysm on colleagues, underlings and, of course, the victims. Throughout the US mainstream media, where these former officials continue to appear regularly, they get solicitous treatment. The presumption of their authority and expertise has barely been dented by their colossal misdeeds—in fact, the disaster has only added to their luster, from the Aspen Festival of Ideas to various Ivy League lecture halls to the Sunday morning network gabfests. As columnist Glenn Greenwald has bitterly noted, the phrase "culture of impunity," routinely applied by Westerners to places like Kenya and Cambodia, is more than apt for official Washington as well, where rules have long ceased to apply.

CIA officers who tortured prisoners violated the Geneva Convention and American law, and to date they have faced no consequences for breaking the rules. They destroyed evidence, shredding records and "misplacing" videos of interrogations that involved torture, and though these acts of defiance have enraged the judiciary, everyone knows the agents will face no penalty. The Obama Administration has thrown its weight around in Italy, Spain and Germany to stifle investigations of CIA officers who may have violated the Geneva Conventions. Rules may be rules for some, but not for CIA interrogators.

Many people thought this would change once Barack Obama assumed office, and many people were wrong. As soon as he stepped into the Oval Office, the new President pledged never to launch any probe, much less prosecution, to hold these figures responsible. "Look forward, not backward" is the slogan: any rules that threaten the high and mighty can be shrugged off. Obama loyalists such as *Nation* magazine columnist Melissa Harris-Perry begged Americans to reconcile with Dick Cheney, as if the power to forgive belonged to Americans, and not to Iraqi victims—a perversion of Christian doctrine that allows the perpetrators to tearfully forgive themselves.[1]

Elite impunity tolerates not even the slightest imputation of guilt. Sensing that the White House does not wish to spend political capital on prosecuting elite lawbreakers, some have proposed an award for the war on terror's various whistleblowers and naysayers—a recognition of those who have upheld honor and the rule of law under stress, and an implicit rebuke to those who buckled. But even this gesture of "positive reinforcement" has been rejected by the Obama administration as insufficiently cautious.

By the time impunity has flowed from the cabinet secretary to the common infantryman, it is only partially depleted. The consequences of the "Haditha Massacre" are a vivid case in point. On November 19, 2005, a group of eight US Marines allegedly killed twenty-four Iraqis, at least fifteen of them civilians, in the western city of Haditha. An IED had killed one Marine and wounded two others earlier in the day, and in retaliation eight troops from the Third Battalion first shot dead nine Iraqi men, whom the soldiers later claimed were insurgents, and then went house-to-house killing civilians with grenades. After a long-delayed investigation, eight Marines were charged a year later: the largest single war-crimes indictment against American troops in Iraq or Afghanistan. But five years after the charges, six of the accused soldiers have seen their charges dismissed, and another was found not guilty. The trial of the their leader, Sergeant Frank Wuterich, has just ended with a guilty plea to a single charge of negligent dereliction of duty, a minor offense that will result in no jail time.[2]

There have been a handful of prosecutions of US soldiers for the cold-blooded killing of Afghan civilians. But in wartime, soldiers who open fire on civilians are unlikely to face any legal consequences. Earlier, I cited Ethan McCord, the infantryman filmed in the "Collateral

Murder" video retrieving wounded children, who recalled his battalion commander ordering troops to issue "360 degree rotational fire" to "kill every [expletive] in the street!"[3] There can be little doubt this order is a violation of the Uniform Code of Military Justice, and of the broadly agreed-upon laws of armed conflict. ("That is absolutely a war crime," David Glazier, an attorney at the National Center for Military Justice told me.) But don't expect an investigation into McCord's old battalion commander. When foreign troops invade and occupy, they enjoy a high degree of immunity until the occupied nation summons the power and the will to deny it to their armed invaders. This immunity to the rule of law is in fact an essential condition for military occupation. It was the Iraqi government's refusal to grant ongoing immunity for US troops that rang a virtual end to the American occupation in late 2011.

None of this is a new development since the American invasions of Afghanistan and Iraq. The My Lai massacre, in which an American battalion killed some 500 Vietnamese civilians in 1968, led not to the enforcement of the Uniform Code of Military Justice's own rules against methodically slaughtering unarmed civilians, but to an official cover-up. Of the twelve officers who were eventually indicted, only one, Lieutenant William Calley, was convicted. He was sentenced to life imprisonment but served three-and-a-half years under house arrest before walking free. Armies are simply not very good at enforcing their own rules against soldiers who slaughter civilians.

No summary of our post-9/11 lawless rampage would be complete without an inventory of the lawyers who approved, encouraged and authorized the misdeeds. John Yoo is the most famous of the attorneys who authorized torture from inside the Office of Legal Counsel; he remains a tenured professor of law at the University of California, Berkeley. Though less famous, the case of Jay Bybee is more chilling: the Office of Legal Counsel attorney who justified various forms of torture in precise, lawyerly detail is now a judge on the US Court of Appeals on the Ninth Circuit, just one layer of authority below the Supreme Court of the United States. And though these lawyers who authorized torture have received criticism, the lawyers at the Departments of State and Defense who wrote up legal rationales for the Iraq War itself go blameless: incredibly, William Howard Taft IV, who as legal adviser to the State Department provided the legal rationale for war, is still considered an "authority" in the field of international law.

If Bradley Manning had launched a war that slaughtered hundreds of thousands; if he had tortured prisoners; if he had shot dead Iraqi civilians: if he were a lawyer, justifying all of the above, or some general or cabinet-level official whispering state secrets to Bob Woodward over a martini— he'd be on easy street.

We lawyers tend to think that law is by nature something good and just and that it's dirty politics that fouls everything up. But the Wikileaks disclosures reveal something far more troubling than violations of the rule of law; they reveal the pathology of the laws themselves. Can it be possible that the Rule of Law is not an unmitigated good? In fact, several of the most appalling atrocities revealed in the leaks are in fact perfectly legal, showing us that the rules and laws of the game are often profoundly problematic, if not downright rotten.

Let us start with the "Collateral Murder" video watched by millions around the world, an unclassified item allegedly leaked by Bradley Manning. To recap, the video shows an Apache gunship opening fire on a group of civilians, including two Reuters News Agency employees, accompanied by a couple of men with weapons; the gunships circle back to shoot the wounded dead; when a van comes in to retrieve the wounded, the gunship shoots it to pieces too. All the while, pilot and crew joke among themselves, a violation of etiquette that has, weirdly, drawn the most condemnation. One might expect that such a graphic atrocity would be fodder for the condemnation of the major human rights organizations—Amnesty International, Human Rights Watch, Human Rights First—who monitor violations of the laws of war.

Not one of these groups has issued a statement on the massacre. Human Rights Watch declined to comment entirely on the incident—in their report on human rights law and international humanitarian law violations in Iraq, published in February 2011, there is no mention of the incident, though it lies well within the timeframe covered by the document. The former policy director for Terrorism, Counterterrorism and Human Rights at Amnesy International USA told me that they had not commented on the incident largely because any report was bound to be muddy and far from clear-cut, given that the law is not at all on one side. Gabor Rona, legal director of Human Rights First, told me that there wasn't enough information to ascertain whether "international humanitarian law," as the laws of armed conflict are euphemistically called, was violated. He told me that Human Rights First had no Freedom of Information Act requests pending for more such information. Why haven't any of the big human rights outfits commented on this sensational and widely known atrocity? Rona told me he didn't know. He seemed a little embarrassed.

Why haven't these human rights groups addressed the most vividly documented incident of the military slaughter of civilians since the My Lai massacre? These human rights experts were certainly as troubled as anyone else by the killing. The media departments of all three nonprofits are always hungry for headlines—it's not as if they, unlike the rest of the world, did not watch the video upon its release in March 2010. The reason for their silence is disquietingly simple: the gunship's actions were, under the Rule of Law as codified and accepted in international humanitarian law (IHL), *perfectly legal.*

Recognition of the massacre's legality can be seen as a defense of the helicopter crew's actions—or as an indictment of the laws of war themselves. As Gary Solis, an expert in the laws of war at Georgetown University painstakingly pointed out in an interview with *Harper's*, the gunship crew's decision is by the letter of the law defensible.[4] Among the civilians there were plainly a few armed men—nobody contests that. There had been insurgent gunfire in the area earlier in the day in that area. We should remember that the laws of war unambiguously permit the killing of civilians, provided that the killing of civilians is proportional to the military advantage pursued; that a reasonable effort is made to distinguish combatant from non-combatant; that the overall objective is a military necessity. (These principles turn out to be remarkably supple when managed by a great power occupying a lesser power.) As for opening fire on the van, this too was legal. "An 'enemy' vehicle without red cross, red crescent, or white flag receives no special protection, even if wounded personnel are on board." The conclusion, however discomfiting to the moral intuition of most humans who have seen the video, is unavoidable. "I believe it unlikely that a neutral and detached investigator would conclude that the helicopter personnel violated the laws of armed conflict. Legal guilt does not always accompany innocent death." It bears noting that Gary Solis is no neoconservative ultra but a seasoned scholar who has taught at the London School of Economics and West Point and is an unhesitant critic of many of the Bush-Cheney Administration's legal distortions.

Many viewers of the video have found it disturbing to consider that the gunship's crew shot dead some dozen civilians and suffered no penalty. This implies an abuse of the system. What many may find more disturbing still is that these soldiers' actions are safely within the zone of legality, and, under the laws of war as we know them, are deserving of no penalty whatsoever. This implies an injustice hardwired within the system of laws itself.

Another of Pfc. Manning's alleged revelations is the widespread torture of Iraqi citizens with the full knowledge of occupying troops. The US Army recounts all kinds of terrible torture and abuse, some of it fatal, meted out to Iraqi prisoners by Iraqi authorities, all with the tacit or explicit knowledge of the occupying powers. Surely this must be a violation of the laws of war?

In fact, the Geneva Conventions are very vague about the responsibilities of occupying troops to ensure the safety of prisoners captured under their watch. Although IHL is very clear that troops have a duty not to torture, the law goes murky when it comes to handing over prisoners to an occupied nation's own authorities. Common Article I of the Fourth Geneva Convention includes only nebulous language about a duty for troops to "ensure respect" for prisoners handed over to a third party. But it is unclear whether this obligation is incurred by the state or by individual troops, and it is foggier still what this obligation actually means. (The vagueness of the Geneva Conventions on this point is no accident: the conferences that have drafted international humanitarian law have had most of their input from occupiers, who tend to be powerful states with lots of political power and clever lawyers.) And in June 2004, a secret "fragmentary order," FRAGO 242, was issued by the Department of Defense itself, ordering coalition troops not to investigate any violation of IHL, including the torture of detainees, unless coalition members were directly involved. If there is Iraqi-on-Iraqi abuse or torture, "only an initial report will be made … No further investigation will be required unless directed by HQ."[5]

It cannot be stressed enough that the above arguments for the legality of the "Collateral Murder" slaughter and the torture of Iraqi citizens are not arguments for these acts' morality or goodness. Both deeds are atrocities, if the word has any meaning. But we need to face the unedifying truth that a wartime atrocity can be unimpeachably *legal*. For many, the prospect of war crimes going unpunished is strangely comforting, as it reaffirms faith in the overall system whose occasional abuses can be dealt with in due time. Such a scenario is more easily swallowed than the prospect of graphic atrocities being perfectly consistent with the laws of war. International Humanitarian Law, after all, is supposed to regulate, restrain and civilize warfare. The truth is that it authorizes and permits violence more often than it prohibits it—as David Kennedy of Harvard Law School has written, "We should be clear: this bold new vocabulary beats ploughshares into swords as often as the reverse."[6] The fantasy of clean warfare is deeply cherished by so much of the Western center-left, the great dream that military violence can be surgical, humanitarian, therapeutic, an instrument of human rights. This has rarely, if ever, proven to be the case.

The laws of war, today as a hundred years ago, are written in favor of occupying armies. Insurgents have no rights today any more than the Comanche and Nez Perce did a century ago. In the late nineteenth century such insurgents were called, with what now seems refreshing candor, "savages"; now they are "non-uniformed unprivileged combatants."[7] The international legal consensus then was that any measure was permitted against such an enemy—a point echoed by the Bush-Cheney Administration's insistence that the prisoners at Guantánamo and Bagram do not enjoy any rights under the laws of armed conflict.

The truth of these revelations is that the laws of war are not a neutral, objective source of morality but a contested battleground itself. Although the International Committee of the Red Cross once served as a powerful arbiter in deciding how these laws were to be interpreted, the ICRC's power has waned. As Claude Bruderlein, director of Harvard's Program on Humanitarian Policy and Conflict Research, told me, "In the 1960s, the

ICRC was the Vatican of international humanitarian law; now there's a form of legal Protestantism, a total fragmentation of the legal community, and everyone reads the laws and interprets them as they please. The ICRC must be careful; if they go after the US for using some weapon that's standard in NATO, then the ICRC will have a coalition arrayed against them."

Like any regulatory scheme, the laws of armed conflict are susceptible to capture. Nor is this some brand-new perversion of international law particular to America's fleeting moment as global overlord. At least since the Dutchman Hugo Grotius, founder of modern international law, published his first legal work in 1604—a legal apologia for his nation's privateers in the East Indies—the laws of war have themselves been a secretion of great power politics. (Grotius later fled his native Netherlands to serve Gustavus Adolphus, King of Sweden, and wrote legal justifications for his client's voracious annexations in northern Germany during the Thirty Years War; according to legend, the warrior king used Grotius' writings as a pillow to sleep on after a hard day's pillage.[8])

Perhaps the pithiest encapsulation of law's devious talent to mask and legitimize military violence belongs to Pfc. Manning himself:

(02:26:01 PM) bradass87: i dont believe in good guys versus bad guys anymore... i only [see] a plethora of states acting in self interest... with varying ethics and moral standards of course, but self-interest nonetheless

(02:26:18 PM) bradass87: s/only/only see/

(02:26:47 PM) info@adrianlamo.com: the tm meant i was being facetious

(02:26:59 PM) bradass87: gotchya

(02:27:47 PM) bradass87: i mean, we're better in some respects... we're much more subtle... use a lot more words and legal techniques to legitimize everything

(02:28:00 PM) bradass87: its better than disappearing in the middle of the night

(02:28:19 PM) **bradass87:** but just because something is more subtle, doesn't make it right

What the Wikileaks documents reveal is something far more disturbing than a few unpunished abuses that the law hasn't gotten around to correcting. What they reveal are the profound failings of the law itself.

Why would we cling to any notion of the Rule of Law? As professor Conor Gearty of the London School of Economics has pointed out, the Rule of Law (along with "human rights") has become a buzzword for Washington's neocolonial venture, just as "civilizing mission" and "pacification of the natives" were talismanic slogans for a previous century's imperialists.[9] We preach the Rule of Law as a get-rich-quick panacea to developing countries—never mind that China, with its ten percent annual GDP growth rates, barely has a legal system; never mind that American courts flouted the Rule of Law whenever it stood in the way of our own industrialization. Why do the great and the good pay such energetic lip service to this concept?

As compromised as the Rule of Law is and has always been, we would do wrong to discard it entirely. Its misty outlines still carry some meaning, and equality before the law remains, as E.P. Thompson put it a generation ago while mulling the same problem, an unalloyed human good. All over the world where violent lawlessness is rife, many see the Rule of Law as far more than mere rhetorical window dressing. From Colombia to Egypt to Italy to Cuba, citizens who risk their lives against the depredations of organized crime or authoritarian states routinely invoke the Rule of Law to give meaning to their acts of resistance. The greatest assault on the Rule of Law comes not from anarchists or left-liberal antinomians who defend Bradley Manning's alleged disclosures. The most powerful intellectual threat to the Rule of Law in the United States today comes from the neoconservative right. More broadly, the threat comes from those who hold themselves above the law and have the power in fact to stay above it.

This is best encapsulated in a recent law review article by Professor Adrian Vermeule, an up-and-comer at Harvard Law School. Vermeule argues that legal black holes—the term was coined by a British law lord expressly for Guantánamo—are not only tolerable but necessary. Any attempt to fill them in with law would be "hopelessly utopian," "quixotic" even. "Our Schmittian Administrative Law," published in 2009 in *The Harvard Law Review*, draws heavily on the work of the jurist Carl Schmitt, a Nazi sympathizer and lifelong opponent of the rule of law and liberal democracy.[10] A figure of fascination among left-wing academics for the cold eye he cast on liberalism's sacred myths, Schmitt's ideas had always been held at a prophylactic distance.

No longer. Schmitt's ready-made conceptual lexicon for political emergencies, non-state combatants, and the need for strident executive authority has proven irresistible to ambitious American intellectuals in the revolving door between federal government and the finer law schools. These tweedy immoralists urge us to relax our square-john commitment to the rule of law and embrace strong executive action. Surely the moralizing banalities of rule-of-law theorists are inadequate for the unique challenges of the post-9/11 global order, they tell us.

But as the events of the past decade plainly show, one would be on safer ground drawing the opposite conclusion about the Rule of Law's value—and its effectiveness in ensuring national security. Our government responded to 9/11 with numerous extraordinary measures contemptuous of ordinary legality, and virtually every one of them has been disastrous in its consequences. From the illegal conquest of Iraq to rampant torture to mass warrantless wiretapping to the military commissions of Guantánamo, these policies have been exorbitantly costly in blood (of many nations, including our own), money, and American prestige. Has any part of our frenzied rejection of legal restraints improved national security? Just how did any of these radical above-the-law measures help the United States, let alone the world?

Vermeule is correct to note that these black holes are likely to dilate rather than contract as an imperialist foreign policy strains our legal system, not only with the panic and fervor of war but with juridical conundrums of extraterritoriality, non-state belligerents, and geographically far-fetched definitions of self-defense. (Drone strikes in Yemen, Somalia and the tribal regions of northwest Pakistan are all rationalized by State Department lawyers on the grounds that they are in "defense" of United States territory.)

Millions voted for Barack Obama because he promised a restoration of something approaching the Rule of Law after the unremitting "emergency" of his predecessor, and its lawless spree of self-inflicted disasters. Instead, the Obama Administration has failed to rethink, much less reform, the extralegal emergency measures installed by George W. Bush, an opinion widely shared not just among civil libertarians but among former Bush-Cheney officials. Filling in the many legal black holes in America might include shutting down Guantánamo (wherever it may be located) and radically rethinking our post-9/11 security policies. The clamp on information that has kept the public ignorant about so many critical foreign policy issues would have to be loosened considerably. Instead, Obama has preserved, streamlined and often intensified his predecessor's bellicose foreign policies, reserving the government's vindictive fury for whistleblowers.

Those of us who defend the alleged deeds of Manning appeal to a sense of justice. We have no choice but to use the language of law in defending him, even if we recognize that such appeals are in vain. A great many of the approximately 700,000 leaked documents are not classified at all; many should be covered by the Whistleblower Protection Act. But many would not be so covered, and Manning—or whoever it was—deserves all the more credit for this act of civil disobedience. It is because he broke the law that we know so much more; it is because he broke the law that we honor him.

Bradley Manning's alleged act was an act of intense political courage. The United States is an increasingly depoliticized society, and we struggle to comprehend the very concept of the political. Instead, our media have tended to see Manning as motivated purely by individual psychology, or by his less-than-ideal childhood and family life, or by his sexual preference and gender identity. All the while, the leaks themselves have furnished the world's most prestigious print media with story after story after story. Instead of protecting their source, major newspapers have been content to label Bradley Manning a headcase.

This is nonsense. Releasing the war logs and the diplomatic cables was a practical solution to a severe problem of government obfuscation. The past ten years have been a costly disaster for American foreign policy—and for the people of Iraq, Afghanistan and Pakistan. Government secrecy and distortion have played a major role in creating this blood-soaked mess. Only with some knowledge can the course be corrected. Manning was perfectly clear about this in his discussion with the informant who turned him in, after telling him that "it was forwarded to WL":

(02:28:10 AM) bradass87: i want people to see the truth... regardless of who they are... because without information, you cannot make informed decisions as a public

(02:28:10 AM) info@adrianlamo.com <AUTO-REPLY>: I'm not here right now

(02:28:50 AM) bradass87: if i knew then, what i knew now... kind of thing...

(02:29:31 AM) bradass87: or maybe im just young, naive, and stupid...

(02:30:09 AM) info@adrianlamo.com: which do you think it is?

(02:30:29 AM) bradass87: im hoping for the former

(02:30:53 AM) bradass87: it cant be the latter

(02:31:06 AM) bradass87: because if it is... were fucking screwed

(02:31:12 AM) bradass87: (as a society)

(02:31:49 AM) bradass87: and i dont want to believe that we're screwed

If the disclosures have failed to alter American statecraft, then the fault lies not with the whistleblower, but with a society incapable of receiving this great gift of knowledge.

7

THE COURT-MARTIAL OF BRADLEY MANNING

What Is the Fate of Pfc. Bradley Manning?

At the time of this writing, Manning's court-martial has been postponed, once again, and is now scheduled for March of 2013—over a thousand days after the defendant's arrest at FOB Hammer. The Uniform Code of Military Justice (UCMJ) specifies that a court-martial must take place no later than 120 days after a soldier's arrest and the Sixth Amendment grants the right to a speedy trial, but these legal protections have not been meaningful.

Of the twenty-two charges against Pfc. Manning, some are relatively minor, like violating Army Regulation 380-5, on the proper storage of classified information. But two in particular are extremely serious. First, the Espionage Act of 1917, though never intended by its authors to be used against domestic leakers and whistleblowers, has been leveled against Manning, just as it has been the basis of six other prosecutions under the Obama administration. (That is more than twice as many as all previous presidents' domestic use of the statute combined.) More serious still is Article 104 of the UCMJ: "Aiding the Enemy," a capital offense. And though the administration has made it clear they will not seek the death penalty, a life sentence is a strong possibility.

How has Pfc. Manning "aided the enemy"? The government has argued in pretrial hearings that because al-Qaeda in the Arabian Peninsula (AQAP) had access to the internet—and therefore to the Wikileaks site— Manning has "aided" them. Leave aside the fact that AQAP also has access to Nike shoes without making the Oregon sportswear company a material supporter of terrorism. The statute comes equipped with an alarmingly broad phrase, "either directly or indirectly": "[A]ny person who ... gives intelligence to or communicates or corresponds with or holds any intercourse with the enemy, either directly or indirectly; shall suffer death or such other punishment as a court-martial or military commission may direct." The implications of convicting Manning for "indirectly" aiding the enemy, without any conscious intent, are enormous. This could become a capital offense if the court rules that the Aiding the Enemy statute is as capacious as the prosecution would like it to be.[1] There are more than a thousand enlisted men and women engaged in blogging, an activity warmly encouraged by top brass as beneficial to morale. Will this suddenly be criminalized? In pretrial hearings, Manning's defense attorney moved for this charge, at once the most serious and the most ridiculous, to be dismissed. Judge Denise Lind ruled against the motion, and the charges currently stand. In pretrial hearings the prosecution indicated it would be using digital media found on Osama bin Laden's laptop as an exhibit—does it contain downloaded Wikileaks material?

Though the court-martial itself has not begun at the time of this writing, the pretrial hearings have revealed the contours of Manning's legal defense. Rather than contest any of the facts, attorney David Coombs (a veteran military lawyer with twelve years of experience in the Judge Advocate General's Corps) is set to argue that extenuating circumstances cast the leaks in a light less unfavorable to Manning.

First, Coombs will show that the leaks, contrary to the government's warnings of bloody battlefield reprisals and diplomatic Armageddon, have done no harm. Coombs has labored mightily to have the post-leak internal damage assessments that were conducted by the State Department, the military and the FBI produced as evidence, and has met with foot-dragging reluctance to dislodge these (no doubt classified) documents. The prosecution has countered that whether the leaks did any damage is immaterial, as consequences (or the lack thereof) are not an element of the lower-level charges brought against Pfc. Manning. Although the judge has agreed with this reasoning, the government's damage reports, which promise to be far milder than the instant panic of so many officials and elite media, are nevertheless likely to come into play in determining Manning's sentence for the more serious charges.

Among the other mitigating factors asserted by the defense is the near-total lack of information security at FOB Hammer, where the Sensitive Compartmented Information Facility was wholly unregulated. If classified material is so loosely guarded, who is to blame? Not to mention that some 854,000 Americans hold top-secret security clearance.[2] How truly "secret" was any of the leaked material?

The most controversial line of defense pursued by Manning's attorney is his insistence that the private did not receive the mental health treatment he needed. It's true that Pfc. Manning did amass a record of infractions throughout his stateside training that gave some of his superiors pause about deploying him to the battlefront in Iraq. He was almost cycled out of basic training at Fort Leonard Wood, was later in trouble for throwing chairs at Fort Drum, and punched a female superior in the face at FOB

Hammer, where he had the bolt from his rifle removed and was demoted. Manning's reasons for seeking a discharge from the military, "gender identity disorder," are taken by many, even liberal-minded people, as *prima facie* evidence of being "deeply troubled."

But to supporters of Bradley Manning who see his alleged leaks as an act of moral sanity, this defense is not entirely welcome. Doesn't it seem to buy in to the way whistleblowers and dissenters are routinely pathologized, psychologized and medicalized? And why should being transgender be seen as a mental illness anyway, rather than another form of normal, a way of being that exists in some manner in most societies? (The American Psychiatric Association announced in December of 2012 that it was narrowing its definition of gender identity disorder to a more rigorously defined "gender dysphoria" in the next edition of its widely used *Diagnostic and Statistical Manual of Mental Disorders*, just as it famously struck homosexuality from its list of mental illnesses in 1973.) Is Manning being betrayed by his own legal defense?

Not remotely. Those who support Manning, including this author, should accept the fact that the legal defense of Bradley-Manning-the-individual and the moral/political defense of Manning-the-cause may have some irreconcilable differences. Of the few legal defenses available, defense attorney Coombs has an obligation to zealously pursue them to get the best possible outcome for his client, who again, is not only a set of causes but a flesh-and-blood human being who faces life in prison. Those who fret, somewhat patronizingly, that Manning is being bullied and intimidated by his attorney into employing this line of defense should remember that the defendant in question has demonstrated a lifetime of fierce independence of mind and of will. That is of course exactly how Pfc. Manning wound up where he is now.

All that said, we should note that neither mental health problems nor gender identity, whatever success these defenses may achieve in lessening the sentence, can explain Manning's alleged deed. Regarding Manning's psychology, the fact that he sought out mental health counseling is by far the most ordinary thing about him. Mental health troubles are pandemic in the US military: the leading cause of death among active-duty US troops over the past four years has been not IEDs or sniper fire but suicide. The US military is rapidly expanding its counseling and mental health services and working overtime to erase the stigma that still attaches to soldiers who seek help.

As for Manning's sexuality, this is surely an important part of the defendant's personal history just as it would be for anyone else. But the matter of sexuality and gender identity are by and large irrelevant to the affair of the leaks. It has been a right-wing talking point that Manning is an example of why gays shouldn't be allowed to serve in the military, tapping into an ageless stream of bigotry that sees all homosexuals as a fifth column of appeasers who sap the national resolve. On the left, some have had made an analogous argument but inflected as a compliment, not an insult: Manning's outsider status must have given him some special empathy with the Iraqi civilians he knew were getting tortured and terrorized under the US occupation.

What both of these viewpoints miss is that Pfc. Manning as a gay man was not remotely unique in the US armed forces. Of the hundreds of thousands of Americans with access to the same secrets that Manning allegedly leaked, we can safely assume that thousands are lesbian, gay, bisexual or transgender. "[H]alf the S2 was at least bi" is Manning's own description of the Army intel unit in which he served at FOB Hammer. Does being gay or transgender really have anything to do with a whistleblower's intense sense of responsibility? Call it the rule of RC squared: for every Roger Casement (the gay subject of the British crown who blew the whistle on atrocities in the Belgian Congo and the Amazon rubber plantations and who was hanged for the cause of Irish independence in 1916), there is a Roy Cohn, the gay right-hand man of anticommunist witch-hunter Joseph McCarthy and one of the nastiest lawyers in postwar US history (portrayed memorably by Al Pacino in the miniseries *Angels in America*). Being gay or transgender does not entail any particular set of views on national security, freedom of information or the morality of war and occupation. (Of the several transgender clients that this author and attorney has had as clients and colleagues in civil rights advocacy, not one has evinced an innate drive to declassify public records.) Manning's sexual preference and gender identity certainly make him easier to marginalize, and his sending a few letters out of the Quantico brig as "Breanna Manning" may well have been part of what led the commanders there to keep him in punitive isolation against all medical advice and their own regulations. (Zinnia Jones, an online interlocutor of Manning from his deployment at Fort Drum, has written an eloquent condemnation of the reflexive tendency to view all transgender people as "troubled."[3]) But even without these homophobic and transphobic reactions, how different would the treatment of Bradley Manning and the public reaction to the leaks have been?

The reader will note that from the title of this book onward I have called the alleged leaker "Bradley" Manning and used masculine pronouns to describe him. This is a considered and deliberate choice, and it takes into account all the known facts: that Manning had investigated gender transition, experimented with cross-dressing and opened a Twitter account as "Breanna Manning." But at the time of this writing, Pfc. Manning has not made any clear and public decision to present himself publicly as anyone other than "Bradley," which according to his lawyer is how he wishes to be addressed. His choices are of course constrained by terrible circumstances, but those are the only circumstances he has. Whether Manning should be addressed as Bradley or Breanna is a choice that belongs to one person and one person alone, not to advocates and supporters, however well-meaning, who have granted themselves the power to speak on another adult's behalf without permission. I discussed this with a transgender former client of mine, someone I had employed while conducting the first-ever empirical investigation into employment discrimination against transgender job-seekers.[4] My former client described the rush of some advocates to effect their own gender-transition on Pfc. Manning as "hyper-corrective," "a projection." "In the absence of any clear coming-out, it seems excessive." When and if Bradley Manning clearly and publicly articulates a wish to be known otherwise, this author, who is listening attentively, will address him or her however he or she wishes.

Many of the outsized issues that collide in this case—gender identity, the competing risks of secrecy and transparency, the Iraq War—are, disconcertingly, only faintly present in the legal battle itself. Some observers, often those who came of age resisting the Vietnam War, have faulted defense attorney Coombs for not blasting out a scorching political defense that puts the prosecution and the entire Iraq War on trial. This is more or less the approach that I have adopted with this book, which I hope will count for something in the court of public opinion. But in an actual court of law such a strategy can only work under very specific political weather conditions, when widespread sympathy for the defendant might coax a jury, along with the media and perhaps the judge, to bend, ignore or even nullify the law. In the year 2013, as far as Bradley Manning goes, such conditions are far from being met, and a jury of military officers is certain not to be swayed by such an approach.

Indeed, the American political climate remains horribly inhospitable to Manning. Over two years after the first release of Manning's alleged leaks, and over eleven years after 9/11, the United States is still in thrall to the politics of fear, a pillar of which is ongoing national panic about leaks. Although there is relatively little debate about the failure of

President Obama's 30,000-troop surge in Afghanistan—of the 2,165 US soldiers killed there, nearly three quarters were killed since 2009, with comparable rises of civilian casualties—both major parties have not ceased to wail about the supposed threat of national security leaks. The aggressive prosecutions of leakers and whistleblowers by the Obama Department of Justice is not just the work of a rogue executive power; there is constant pressure and demand steadily emanating from Congress for exactly such prosecutions. In the summer of 2012, congressional fury about new leaks reached a frenzied pitch after the *New York Times* ran articles containing classified information about drone strikes and a cyberwarfare program, culminating in the Democratic and Republican leadership of the intelligence subcommittees in the Senate and the House giving a press conference to denounce insufficient government secrecy, with Republican Senator John McCain scarcely outdone by Democratic Senator Dianne Feinstein.[5] All the while, other voices, often within the US government itself, have released report after report on the brokenness of the classification system and the heavy risks of such extreme secrecy— most recently by the Public Interest Declassification Board set up by Congress.[6] Alas, these voices are nearly drowned out by the nonstop baying of elite officials for ever greater secrecy and harsher clampdowns on leaks.

Another barometer of anti-leak panic is Washington's never-ending legal quest for the head of Julian Assange, Wikileaks' founder. When Assange took refuge in the Ecuadorean embassy in London in June of 2012, many mocked his flight as mere theatrics and pooh-poohed his fears of being shipped off to the United States for trial. But these fears are entirely well-founded. We know as a fact that a grand jury in Alexandria, Virginia, has been empaneled to explore criminal charges against Assange and Wikileaks. The only question is whether they have delivered an indictment.[7] According to documents released by Canberra after a freedom-of-information request, the Australian foreign service has been preparing in consultation with Washington for the day when Assange is extradited to the United States.[8] This remains a very real possibility should he be sent to Sweden to face charges of sexual misconduct, protestations of Scandinavian rectitude aside. (In the decade after 9/11, Sweden amassed an appalling record of handing over foreign nationals to Washington's client states for torture and interrogation, as has been documented by Human Rights Watch and other monitors.[9])

Given this climate, can Pfc. Bradley Manning hope to get any kind of justice in a military court? Many observers have assumed that a civilian court would be fairer and more lenient, but this assumption does not withstand scrutiny. First, civilian courts have often been just as harsh—even harsher—in their sentencing of national security defendants than some of the military tribunal trials at Guantánamo. (This is not a defense of that deeply flawed court system which deserves to be shut down for any number of important reasons.) But consider the amazing fifteen-year sentence handed by a federal court to college student Syed Fahad Hashmi for letting a "friend" store raincoats and socks that were supposedly destined for a terrorist training camp in Hashmi's apartment. (Hashmi spent three years in pretrial solitary confinement.) By contrast, the Gitmo tribunals' first conviction resulted in a time-served sentence of five and a half years for Salim Hamdan, Osama bin Laden's chauffeur.

If anything, a court-martial might be kinder to Pfc. Manning than a civilian court. "A military court-martial is, in my opinion the best courtroom that Bradley Manning could go to," said defense attorney Coombs at his first public statement the night of December 3, 2012, at a Unitarian church in Washington. Juries, comprised of officers who have earned at least a bachelor's degree, are typically better educated than juries in the civilian system; military jurors are very likely to have spent time abroad, which for soldiers as for civilians tends to broaden the mind;

members of the "blue-ribbon panel" (as it is called) often take their duty as jurors more seriously than their counterparts in a state or federal court. Coombs also pointed out that military judges have nearly all worked as both prosecutors and defense attorneys, which according to Coombs in his legal experience in both systems, makes military judges more fair-minded. As for the rules of evidence in a court-martial, they are essentially the same as in federal court. None of this is to say that a military jury—which requires a two-thirds vote of its members to convict—will acquit Pfc. Manning, which is highly unlikely. But the court-martial will be certainly no worse for this defendant than a federal court.

By November of 2012, the defense was taking the first step in the delicate dance that might lead to a plea agreement. On November 7, defense attorney Coombs announced that his client was willing to "accept responsibility for offenses that are encapsulated within, or are a subset of, the charged offenses," and asked the court to weigh the legality of this offer. Though not a plea deal in itself, this admission of the *facts* of the lesser offense—but not guilt—could lead to some of the more serious charges (violation of the Espionage Act) being dropped. The government has invested so much in this case that dropping the most serious charge, aiding the enemy, seems most unlikely.

Pretrial hearings have been underway since December 2011—but you might not know it given the scant mainstream media coverage. In part this is because the government is not making media coverage easy; just getting on to Fort Meade, where the trial action is taking place, is a small ordeal with searches under the hood of any journalist's car and a baroque security process for entrance—made slower by power outages which are disturbingly common on a base that also holds the headquarters of the NSA. The government has forbidden electronic recording devices in the courtroom and refuses to make transcripts of the proceedings, another obstacle to journalistic coverage of this important case. The Center for

Constitutional Rights has filed a lawsuit to make courtroom records available, representing a swath of journalists including this author, but so far this push, though expertly conducted by attorney Shayana Kadidal, has not succeeded. The military reasoned that because one Manning solidarity activist, Alexa O'Brien, had shown a near-preternatural skill to manually transcribe the proceedings, there was no need to make any court records public.

Even so, the lack of mainstream media coverage is eerie given that Manning is the source for thousands of major news stories in the past few years. That the *New York Times* didn't bother to send a reporter to cover the first hearings on Manning's pretrial isolation confinement—a subject both sensational and significant—is truly jaw-dropping. Even the neoliberal *New Republic*, no great friend of Wikileaks, scored points off the *Times*' conspicuous absence from Fort Meade, provoking the paper's public editor to rebuke the omission. Days later, the paper sent reporter Scott Shane to cover half a day's worth of the hearing of December 7, 2102, which resulted in a single short article that, according to whistleblower defense attorney Jesselyn Radack of the Government Accountability Project, suffered badly from lack of context.[10] (The seasoned chief US correspondent of the *Guardian*, Ed Pilkington, has by contrast been a fixture at the hearings.)

And so for ten days in late November and early December, the Fort Meade court heard the defense's motion to dismiss all charges on the basis of unlawful pretrial punishment. There was never any chance that this motion would succeed—not unless presiding judge Denise Lind wanted to be transferred to the Aleutian Islands in time for the Christmas holiday—but the motion also requested that Manning's days in punitive isolation count as hard time served at the ratio of ten to one. The hearings also afforded the defense a chance to gain ground on what is likely to become the most important front of this long-term legal battle: public opinion.

The defense began with Captain William Hocter, the brig psychiatrist, who testified that he had repeatedly advised taking Manning off prevention of injury (POI) watch and suicide watch, and that brig leadership repeatedly ignored him. "It was clear to me they'd made up their mind on a course of action and my recommendations had no impact."[11] Two other psychiatrists testified that they too had diagnosed Manning as not being at any risk of self-harm. But Hocter and the others' expert medical opinions were consistently overruled. Manning remained isolated in an eight-by-six-foot cell for nine months, at least twenty-three hours a day.

Master Sergeant Craig Blenis, who carried the title of "counselor" told the court he found Manning a little "arrogant" for turning down invitations to play chess with him or do "brainteasers."[12] Blenis seems to have had his feelings bruised by the solitary detainee. On December 13, 2010, a package arrived at Quantico for Manning—most likely a birthday gift arriving four days early, as the prisoner had told MSgt. Blenis he was expecting such from his family. But MSgt. Blenis then rejected the package without telling Manning, explaining in an email to his commanding officer that the relative who had mailed it wasn't found on the list of approved senders—the "counselor" adding also that "we just felt like being dicks" as a further justification. Blenis carefully noted that a few days later Manning was taciturn, perhaps upset that his family had forgotten his birthday.

Did Manning's sexual identity sway his jailers against him? On March 2, 2011, when the Quantico officials began confiscating Manning's underwear every night, MSgt. Blenis sent an email to his subordinates instructing them to take the prisoner's "panties" away from him "right before he lays down." The nightly confiscation of Manning's underwear was apparently a laugh riot among the jailers. Quantico's chief legal officer and resident wit Lt. Col. Christopher Greer even emailed Dr. Seuss doggerel about the underwear confiscation to staff. ("I can wear them in a box. I can wear them with a fox. I can wear them in the day. I can wear them so I say. But I can't wear them at night. My comments gave the staff a fright.") When the detainee sent out a letter as "Breanna Manning," this was, in the opinion of Blenis, a sign of mental unwellness and possible suicidal tendencies. And so Blenis recommended consistently that Manning be kept in solitary where he could be closely observed.

On December 6, Chief Warrant Officer 4 James Averhart, brig commander until January 2011, took the stand to explain why he had decided to keep Manning in maximum security as a suicide risk against medical advice. True, US Navy regulations hold that "[w]hen prisoners are no longer considered to be suicide risks by a medical officer, they shall be returned to appropriate quarters." But CWO4 Averhart told the court that the word "shall" in the regulation did not mean "immediately shall," and in fact granted him, as the brig commander, the authority to keep Manning in isolation as he saw fit regardless of what the psychiatrists thought about the prisoner's risk of suicide. And though Averhart said he considered removing Manning from POI watch at least five times, "something always would happen." What exactly always would happen he did not specify. Averhart also said—and he was not the only one— that he felt ninety days would have been optimal for Manning's pretrial confinement, which went on for nine months at Quantico, in maximum custody. Averhart expressed dismay that Manning had for months been kept in leg restraints during his daily hour of "exercise" outside his cell. CWO4 Averhart also described the prisoner as "always courteous."

When Chief Warrant Officer 2 Denise Barnes, who had succeeded CWO4 Averhart as brig commander in January 2012, took the stand on December 8 and 10, she told the court she was reluctant to mix Manning in with the other prisoners in the brig, as they were "really patriotic" (as opposed, presumably, to Manning) and they "knew why he was in there." Not that CWO2 Barnes had any animus against whistleblowers herself;

she averred that she didn't "have a problem with people reporting things up the chain, whether they call it whistleblowing or whatever." However she did "take it personal when people say I have something personal against Manning or another detainee."

But the questioning returned once again to the prisoner's undergarments. It was CWO2 Barnes who made the decision to have Manning stripped naked every night after he had remarked sarcastically that he didn't know where the maximum security constraints on his cell would end, given that he could always find a way to kill himself with his underwear waistband or his flip-flops. And so on March 2, Manning was stripped of his underwear every night and made to stand at attention every morning either nude or wearing a towel. His glasses were also confiscated. In the course of her testimony, Barnes made it clear she considered Blenis' "panties" comments unprofessional but not significant, and that she herself prefers the term "underwear." Lt. Col. Troy Wright, of the security and law enforcement section of the Marine Corps headquarters, notified CWO2 Barnes via email that she had no authority to have the prisoner's underwear removed, but she brushed this off as just a "difference of professional opinion."

December 10 was closing statements. Defense counsel Coombs closed by putting the brig on trial, accusing Blenis and two other guards of perjury and condemning the atmosphere of casual homophobia and intolerance. "If the brig could have put Manning in a straitjacket and padded room, they would have done that." He accused the brig officials of casually mistreating Manning to prevent any recriminations from their superiors. "The fact that Manning's spirit is not broken is amazing," Coombs said. "Being treated as a zoo animal for that period of time has to weigh heavily on the psyche."

In response, chief prosecutor Maj. Ashden Fein conceded Manning had been held improperly under POI watch—but only for seven days out of his nine-month stay. Fein proposed that a 1:1 ratio be applied to this gratuitous spell in isolation, and that the seven days be removed from any eventual sentence. (Fein also commented, tellingly, that "[w]hen brig officials saw someone who was not like others, they tried to figure it out to the best of their abilities on a daily basis.") Manning's supporters found Fein's offer of a seven-day discount less than gracious. "The U.S. government argues that Manning should be sentenced to the rest of his life in prison … minus seven days," tweeted Nathan Fuller of the Bradley Manning Support Network. At the time of this writing, Judge Denise Lind is deliberating over how much time served to grant Pfc. Manning. What remains to be seen is how much of Manning's isolation torture was a conscious and directed attempt to break him and make him implicate Julian Assange, and how much was just the ordinary doltish cruelty of American prisons and, increasingly, of American schools and airports as well.

But the highlight of this round of pretrial hearings, however, was another witness. On November 30, Pfc. Bradley Manning himself took the stand to describe his arrest in Iraq and confinement there, in Kuwait for a month, and in the Quantico brig. And after over a year of silence, filled by many others speaking about him and for him, his own voice was heard.

Pfc. Manning said that after being held in cage-like cells in Iraq and Kuwait, he was "elated" to get back to American soil.

After a few days at Quantico he requested new underwear "because no matter how often they were washed they still had the smell of Iraq on them."

Manning said he had turned down the offer of a Bible, and had requested from a guard Howard Zinn's *A People's History of the United States.*

Manning told the court that when his family came to visit, he didn't like to complain about conditions in the brig, as he didn't want to worry them.

For the court, Pfc. Manning donned the "suicide smock" he was made to wear after March 2 until his transfer out of the isolation cell.

Occasionally he was allowed to read a book his family had sent him. "I read a lot of philosophy, a lot of history. I'm more of a nonfiction reader though I like realistic fiction like John Grisham. Richard Dawkins would be an interesting author."

"The most entertaining thing in there was the mirror. You can interact with yourself. I spent a lot of time with that mirror." This got a laugh.

Manning said that everything he did to show his mental and spiritual fitness and well-being was seized on by brig authorities as a reason to keep him in isolation.

According to many in attendance, Manning seemed calm, self-aware, articulate and intelligent.

Pfc. Manning also told the court how he would try to get a glimpse of real sunlight from his windowless cell by looking through a crack under the door to see a small rectangle of light reflected from a skylight off the door down the hall.

———————

High-profile defenders of Pfc. Manning, most of them non-American, have steadily been coming out in support of the imprisoned whistleblower: Nobel Prize winners Mairead Maguire, Desmond Tutu and Adolfo Pérez Esquivel; rocker and activist Roger Waters; evolutionary biologist Richard Dawkins; and, as always, Daniel Ellsberg. In December of 2012 the accused private won the *Guardian* newspaper's "Person of the Year" vote for the second year running. None of this slow buildup of international support will divert the likely outcome of Manning's court-martial.

From the start it has been a foregone conclusion that Pfc. Manning would be convicted of many of the twenty-two charges against him and sentenced to at least forty years. This is less an example of sound and reasonable laws being twisted or improperly manipulated (though there has been some of that), than the inexorable outcome of a system of laws and incentives expressly designed to foster extreme official secrecy and mass public ignorance. The struggle to free Bradley Manning will be long-term and not dissimilar to the campaigns to pardon or at least retry Leonard Peltier and Mumia Abu-Jamal. The long-term struggle for clemency and justice for Bradley Manning will have to learn from these movements, both their successes and failures. We also have to face the grim truth that given a golden opportunity to free Peltier at the end of his second term, President Bill Clinton instead splurged his political capital on pardoning a felonious crude-oil trader whose wife was a major Democratic Party fundraiser, Marc Rich. With this track record, aggravated by the perennial drive to outflank the Republicans to the right on national security, there is no reason to expect any Democratic president in the foreseeable future to stick out her or his neck for clemency in this case.

Why has the intellectual class that embraced Daniel Ellsberg forty years ago largely shunned Bradley Manning? After all, the only *legal* difference between the two mega-leaks is that every single page of the Pentagon Papers was classed "top secret" whereas not a single one of the Wikileaks documents is of that highest rank of secrecy. Anyone calling for the prosecution of Manning is also calling for the law to be applied against Daniel Ellsberg, who was never acquitted in the mistrial that ended Team Nixon's ham-handed efforts to silence him. (Ellsberg recently noted that the *New York Times* also made it clear that they would not lift a finger to help him with his own criminal defense, and that many of the paper's editors viewed him as a traitor.[13])

The difference between the two cases is of course not legal at all but entirely political. Ellsberg's leaks came at the high-water mark of American liberalism; Manning's during the ongoing rightward drift in security and defense policy. Ellsberg was the ideal whistleblower for public consumption: a former model Marine officer with a distinguished career as a defense analyst; Manning is a twenty-two-year-old private first class, gay and five-foot-two. The enemy in the Vietnam War presented no threat to the US mainland, and the Viet Cong's demand of anticolonial national independence was intelligible, and to a minority of Americans, perfectly legitimate. Washington's enemy today, a vaguely defined "al-Qaeda and affiliates," killed thousands of Americans on native soil; the very notion that Islamist militants might have demands or grievances beyond homicidal mania is too controversial for many public forums.

But the greatest change is the contemporary absence of any shared burden in making war. Throughout the American war in Southeast Asia, there was at least a theoretical possibility that the sons, brothers and grandsons of policy and media elites might be drafted to fight and to die. It was of course easy enough for middle- and upper-class young men to get draft deferments and exemptions, but back in the time of Dan Ellsberg, the specter of the Vietnam War still sat down at every kitchen table in the country. For the Americans who ran the media, the law schools, the advocacy groups, even government, the chance of Junior coming home damaged by the war, or not coming home at all, was a nagging reality test. But ever since Nixon abolished the military draft in 1973, the American middle and upper class have by and large had no skin in the game when it comes to making war. In fact Bush-Cheney's two wars have come with tax *cuts*, and the only shared sacrifice asked of the nation is the pointless and annoying removal of one's shoes in airport security. The sense of urgency that led many American elites to champion Ellsberg is wholly absent today now that the ranks are filled exclusively with volunteers, for the most part from families without much wealth, connections or political clout. Volunteers, in other words, like Pfc. Bradley Manning. For US political and media elites, military conflict is as dreamily abstract as the war porn once screened around the clock at FOB Hammer, now abandoned by the US army and falling apart deep in the Mada'in Qada desert. In the United States, the great and the good have been very happy to turn their backs on Bradley Manning and his scandalous disclosures.

But who is the responsible and ethical citizen and who are the havocking narcissists?

THIS MODERN WORLD

by TOM TOMORROW

Panel 1:
CANDIDATE OBAMA SAID WHISTLE-BLOWERS WERE *PATRIOTS* WHO SHOULD BE *ENCOURAGED!*

AND RIGHTLY SO! WITHOUT WHISTLEBLOWERS, WE'D HAVE NEVER LEARNED ABOUT *ABU GHRAIB* OR *WARRANTLESS WIRETAPPING!*

Panel 2:
BUT THE OBAMA ADMINISTRATION HAS ALL BUT DECLARED *WAR* ON WHISTLEBLOWERS!

THEY'VE INVOKED THE *ESPIONAGE ACT* IN FIVE CASES-- WHICH, AS JANE MAYER NOTES IN THE NEW YORKER, IS MORE TIMES "THAN HAVE OCCURRED IN ALL PREVIOUS ADMINISTRATIONS *COMBINED!*"

Panel 3:
IN THAT SAME ARTICLE, A CONSERVATIVE POLITICAL SCIENTIST--WHO *SUPPORTS* MORE STRINGENT PROTECTION OF CLASSIFIED MATERIAL-- DECLARES THAT "OBAMA HAS PRESIDED OVER THE MOST DRACONIAN CRACKDOWN ON LEAKS IN OUR HISTORY--EVEN MORESO THAN *NIXON!*"

RIBBIT!

Panel 4:
AND YALE LAW PROFESSOR JACK BALKIN SAYS THAT "WE ARE WITNESSING THE BIPARTISAN NORMALIZATION AND LEGITIMIZATION OF A *NATIONAL SURVEILLANCE STATE!*"

I GUESS THESE THINGS JUST SNEAK UP ON YOU SO GRADUALLY SOMETIMES, YOU DON'T EVEN REALIZE WHAT'S *HAPPENING* 'TIL IT'S TOO LATE.

Panel 6:
YOU KNOW, IT'S ACTUALLY A *MYTH* THAT FROGS WILL REMAIN IN A POT OF SLOWLY-HEATED WATER UNTIL THEY BOIL TO DEATH.

COME *BACK* HERE! YOU'RE SPOILING A *PERFECTLY GOOD METAPHOR!*

TOM TOMORROW © 2011 ... www.thismodernworld.com ... twitter.com/tomtomorrow

CHRONOLOGY

December 17, 1987: Bradley Manning is born in Crescent, Oklahoma, a small and heavily Evangelical town in the north central part of the state. His father, Brian Manning, works as an information technology manager for Hertz Rent-a-Car in Oklahoma City. Manning's mother, née Susan Fox, is a Welsh woman whom Brian Manning met and married while deployed in the US Navy (with a classified security clearance) at Cawdor Barracks, Wales.

1990s: Bradley Manning wins three consecutive science fairs at Crescent's K-12 school and is a member of the student team representing Crescent at academic competitions across Oklahoma. He teaches himself HTML and designs his own website at age ten.

2002: Susan Fox and Brian Manning divorce, and Bradley Manning moves with his mother to Haverfordwest in her native Wales, where he enrolls in local schools and joins a computer club.

2005: Bradley Manning surprises his semi-estranged father by calling from Wales and asking if to move in with him and his second wife at their home in Tulsa, Oklahoma. Manning is in London renewing his passport during the terror attacks on the London underground of July 7, 2005. Manning's father sets his son up with a job at a local software company, which Manning, who is 17, is unable to hold down.

2006–2007: After fighting with his father and stepmother, he leaves their home and drifts from Tulsa to Chicago, working a series of low-wage jobs and living out of his car. In mid-2007 he moves in with an aunt in Potomac, Maryland where he works both in retail clothing and as a Starbucks barista.

October 2007: Bradley Manning enlists in the United States Army and is sent for basic training to Fort Leonard Wood, Missouri. Manning, who is 5' 2" and weighs 115 pounds, is routinely picked on by both drill sergeants and fellow enlistees. "There are two kinds of short guys; the kinds who'll take your head off if you mess with them and the kind who gets bullied. Brad Manning was the second kind," says a Fort Leonard Wood contemporary. Manning is placed in the "discharge unit" for enlistees about to be rejected by the Army, where he is bullied further. In the end, faced with low recruitment figures and in urgent need of soldiers with IT skills, the Army decides to "recycle" Manning back into active service for training as an intelligence analyst.

August 2008: After intelligence training at Fort Huachuca, Arizona, Manning is deployed to Fort Drum in upstate New York in the 2nd Brigade Combat Team, 10th Mountain Division. There Manning's superiors record his throwing chairs and screaming at higher-ranking soldiers in his unit. Manning develops a romantic relationship with Brandeis University sophomore Tyler Watkins, whom he visits in Boston on weekend leave.

October 10, 2009: Bradley Manning is deployed to Iraq to work as an intelligence analyst at Forward Operating Base Hammer, one of the most isolated bases in the Iraq theater, located some thirty-five miles east of Baghdad in the Mada'in desert. Manning works as an intelligence analyst in the base's Sensitive Compartmentalized Information Facility, or SCIF. He has access to SIPRNET, the Secret Internet Protocol Router Network, used by the Defense Department and the State Department to transfer classified data, and JWICS, the Joint Worldwide Intelligence Communications System.

November 12, 2009: Manning is promoted to the rank of specialist with a top secret security clearance.

November 2009–April 2010: In the course of his intelligence duties at FOB Hammer, Manning investigates the detention of fifteen Iraqi citizens by the Iraqi Federal Police for printing "anti-Iraqi literature," namely, a pamphlet decrying corruption in their government titled "Where did the money go?" Manning has qualms about peaceful activists being detained by the Iraqi authorities, whose practice of torturing prisoners has been comprehensively documented by the US military. When he brings his concerns up the chain of command, his superior tells him to "shut up" and think about how they can help the Iraqi Federal Police round up more detainees.

Late 2009: On the SIPRNet database, Manning finds the video footage in a Judge Advocates General officer's folder that will later be released by Wikileaks as the "Collateral Murder" video. According to Manning, there are "about two dozen more where that came from."

December 2009: A supervising master sergeant has the bolt from Manning's rifle removed out of concerns over the intelligence analyst's mental health.

April 5, 2010: Wikileaks releases a video filmed from the gunsight of a US Army helicopter that records the crew opening fire on and killing at least 14 Iraqis, including several children and two Reuters employees, and wounding several other civilians, in a suburb of Baghdad on July 12, 2007. The video, called "Collateral Murder," becomes a global sensation.

April 2010: Renowned hacker and convicted felon Adrian Lamo is involuntarily institutionalized in Sacramento, California for nine days.

May 7, 2010: Manning is demoted from Specialist to Private First Class after punching a female superior officer in the face.

May 21, 2010: Bradley Manning commences an instant message dialogue with Adrian Lamo. Over four days, Manning tells Lamo about his childhood, family life, sexual orientation and gender identity; the disclosures he has made to Wikileaks and his relationship with the organization; his motives for leaking the files, citing in its entirety a 1919 *New York Times* editorial on the virtues of "open diplomacy." Two days into the chat, Lamo contacts federal authorities. For the rest of his chats with Manning, Lamo is working as an informant.

May 29, 2010: Manning is arrested by military police and imprisoned in Kuwait.

July 5, 2010: Manning is charged with violating the Espionage Act of 1917, a statute designed originally to punish spies but used with increasing frequency to punish whistleblowers. The Obama administration prosecutes more cases under this act than all previous administrations combined.

July 25, 2010: Wikileaks releases the "Afghan War Logs" to *The Guardian*, *Der Spiegel* and the *New York Times*. 75,000 of the 91,731 files are available on the Wikileaks website; the rest are withheld to minimize risk of harm to individuals named in the documents. Military officials and many journalists condemn the release of the names of some Afghan nationals who have worked with the International Security Assistance Force.

July 29, 2010: Manning is moved from Kuwait to Quantico Marine Corps Base in northeastern Virginia, where he is placed in maximum security detention under prevention of injury watch; in other words, solitary confinement.

September 2010: The Department of Defense admits they have no evidence of Afghan nationals being targeted by the Taliban for collaborating with ISAF forces.

September 27, 2010: At the launch of his new Christmas-themed children's book, *Can't Wait till Christmas*, Mike Huckabee, former governor of Arkansas, former Republican presidential candidate and an evangelical pastor, pauses from book-signing to recommend that Bradley Manning be executed.

October 22, 2010: Wikileaks releases the "Iraq War Logs," 391,832 documents, onto its website. The logs, based on "SigAct" field reports of individual incidents, document the widespread use of torture by Iraqi authorities; a civilian death toll estimate, which the Pentagon had previously denied doing; a tally of Iraqis shot at military checkpoints by US and allied troops, among many other from-the-field reports of the war and occupation. Like the Afghan War Logs, these records make a pointillist portrait of the US invasion and occupation of Iraq.

November 8, 2010: Wikileaks begins the slow release of 251,287 classified US State Department cables. Instead of making most of the documents available at once on its website, Wikileaks releases the documents in a trickle to chosen newspapers and magazines whose editors redact the documents, editing out information that could put innocent people at risk. The documents reveal, among many other things, the American embassy's role in suppressing minimum wage legislation in Haiti; the nepotistic corruption of the Ben Ali family in Tunisia; and a request that Department of State employees covertly gather biometric, credit card and other personal information from foreign diplomats. More than half the leaked cables are not classified; 6% are classed as "secret."

November 29, 2010: Republican Representative Peter King, a longtime supporter of the Irish Republican Army, calls for the US Attorney General to designate Wikileaks a terrorist organization and to prosecute Julian Assange for espionage and treason. The same day, US Secretary of State Hillary Clinton declares these disclosures to be "not just an attack on America's foreign policy interests" but "an attack on the international community."

November 30, 2010: The Office of Career Services at Columbia University's School of International and Public Affairs sends an email to students warning them that if they post about Wikileaks on their Twitter or Facebook, it may deter prospective employers from hiring them.

December 1, 2010: The neoconservative *National Review* publishes an article condemning Manning's pretrial detention in solitary confinement.

December 16, 2010: MIT computer researcher David House tells *The Guardian* that in his twice-monthly visits to Manning at Quantico he has noted a marked deterioration in his friend's focus and mental faculties.

December 19, 2010: Vice President Joseph Biden calls Assange a "high-tech terrorist."

January 20, 2011: David C. Macmichael, former Commander of Headquarters Company at Quantico, writes letter condemning Manning's treatment in detention.

January 23, 2011: Manning's friend David House and journalist Jane Hamsher are turned away from visiting Manning at Quantico.

January 26, 2011: Manning's lawyer, David E. Coombs, reveals that the Quantico base psychiatrist has for months determined that there is no medical rationale for keeping Bradley Manning in solitary confinement.

March 1, 2011: Manning receives a second set of charges, again including the allegation that he violated the Espionage Act of 1917.

March, 2, 2011: Manning comments to guards that the POI restrictions on him are useless as he could still kill himself with the elastic waistband if he really wanted to. Prison authorities subsequently deprive Manning of his underwear at night, forcing him to stand to attention naked every morning at 5 AM.

March 10, 2011: US State Department spokesperson P.J. Crowley says in a press conference that the treatment of Manning at Quantico is "ridiculous and counterproductive and stupid and I don't know why the DoD [Department of Defense] is doing it." Crowley resigns two days later.

March 11, 2011: President Obama is asked at a press conference about the treatment in detention of Bradley Manning. Obama assures reporters that he has looked into it, and that the punitive regime of solitary confinement is for the prisoner's own safety.

March 19, 2011: Ann Clwyd, British member of parliament for Cynon Valley, Wales, condemns the pretrial detention of Manning and calls on her government to raise the issue with US counterparts. "It's just a shame—it's more than a shame, it's a disgrace really that he is being treated like he is," says John Broughton, former Deputy head teacher at the school Manning attended in Wales. "It really is fairly shameful that the British government isn't doing anything about one of its own citizens."

April 11, 2011: Over 250 law school professors, including Obama's Harvard Law School mentor, Laurence Tribe, sign a letter condemning the pretrial solitary confinement of Bradley Manning as "degrading and inhumane conditions that are illegal and immoral."

April 12, 2011: The German Bundestag's human rights committee sends a letter to President Obama condemning the treatment of Bradley Manning at Quantico.

April 20, 2011: Nearly nine months after being placed in solitary confinement, Manning is transferred from Quantico to the Joint Regional Corrections Facility at Fort Leavenworth where he is placed in the communal, medium-security population.

April 21, 2011: At a $5,000-a-plate Democratic Party fundraiser at the St. Regis Hotel in San Francisco addressed by President Obama, a table of ten donors stands up and interrupts the proceedings with a song about Bradley Manning. When they confront the President, his filmed response to them is "He broke the law."

June 7, 2011: Daniel Ellsberg, former US Marine captain and leaker of the Pentagon Papers, declares Bradley Manning a hero and praises his alleged disclosures.

July 1, 2011: 6,600 prisoners held in solitary confinement in Pelican Bay go on hunger strike demanding improvements to their condition. Over 25,000 prisoners remain in some form of long-term solitary confinement in US federal prisons.

July 12, 2011: The United Nations Special Rapporteur on Torture, Juan Mendez, expresses concerns that the Obama administration had denied his request for an unsupervised visit with Manning.

July 13, 2011: *Wired* magazine releases the complete instant chatlogs between Manning and Adrian Lamo, the hacker and informer who turned him in to military authorities.

September 2, 2011: Wikileaks releases all 251,287 State Department cables in unredacted form. The cables had long been available after *Guardian* journalist David Leigh published the secret password to the cache, believing it to be only temporary; the security breach had been vocally advertised by disgruntled former Wikileaks member Daniel Domscheit-Berg. State Department spokesperson Victoria Nuland condemns the leaks as "irresponsible, reckless and frankly dangerous" and alleges they jeopardize the security of foreign nationals revealed to have cooperated with the US government.

September 11, 2011: An Associate Press investigation surveys a broad sample of State Department foreign national sources whose identities were revealed by the unredacted cables. The investigations finds that no harm has been done to any of the sources surveyed, many of whom were surprised to learn that their communications had ever been seen as a state secret.

December 16–23, 2011: Article 32 Hearing to determine if there is sufficient evidence for the charges against Pfc. Manning is conducted over six days at Fort Meade, Maryland. Of the twenty-two charges, eight are for violation of the Espionage Act and one is for Aiding the Enemy, which carries a maximum penalty of death or life without parole. In the course of the hearing's six days, attorney David Coombs does not once seek to deny the alleged deeds. Instead, defense strategy is to spread responsibility for the leaks upward through the chain of command due to the military's failure both to properly secure the classified material and to provide Manning with mental health counseling. Coombs concludes his statement by arguing that the damage done to national interests by the leaks has been minimal: "Where is the damage? [...] The sky has not fallen, and the sky will not fall." The investigating officer denies the defense's request for thirty-six out of thirty-eight witnesses.

January 12, 2012: Investigating officer Lt. Col. Paul Almanza concludes that there is sufficient evidence for Pfc. Manning to face all twenty-two charges in a court-martial.

February 3, 2012: Military District of Washington commander Maj. Gen. Michael Linnington clears the final procedural hurdle by referring all charges against Pfc. Bradley Manning to a general court-martial.

THIS MODERN WORLD

by TOM TOMORROW

ENDNOTES

War casualty figures are drawn from the Costs of War project of the Watson Institute at Brown University, www.costsofwar.org.

Access to the Afghan War Logs, Iraq War Logs, State Department Cables and Guantánamo Files is available at Wikileaks and mirror sites, and on the *Guardian*'s website.

The complete chatlogs between Bradley Manning and Adrian Lamo are available at Wired.com.

Defense lawyer David Coombs' updates about his client Bradley Manning's case and condition are taken from his law firm website, www. armycourtmartialdefense.com.

Chapter 1. A Medal for Bradley Manning

1. Eisenhower Study Group, *The Costs of War Since 2001: Iraq, Afghanistan, and Pakistan*, Providence, RI: Watson Institute for International Study, 2011, 4.

2. Scott Horton, "The El-Masri Cable," *Harper's*, November 29, 2010.

3. Dan Coughlin and Kim Ives, "Wikileaks Haiti: Let Them Live on $3 a Day," *Nation*, June 1, 2011.

4. Daniel Patrick Moynihan, *Secrecy: The American Experience*, New Haven, CT: Yale University Press, 1998, 1.

5. *2011 Report to the President*, Washington DC: Information Security Oversight Office, 2011, 1, at www.archives.gov.

6. Steven Aftergood, "NSA Declassified 200 Year Old Report," *Secrecy News*, June 9, 2011.

7. George Herring, "My Years with the CIA," address given at the January 1997 meeting of the American Historical Association and published in the May 1997 newsletter of the Organization of American Historians, republished on the *Secrecy News* website.

8. Scott Shane, "Complaint Seeks Punishment for Overclassification of Documents," *New York Times*, August 1, 2011.

9. Tim Mak, "McCain: I Didn't Want Arms for Qadhafi," *Politico*, August 29, 2011.

10. US State Department cable 08MANAMA541, August 13, 2008.

11. Maha Azzam, "How Wikileaks Helped Fuel Tunisian Revolution," *CNN*, January 18, 2011.

12. Interview with the author, August 7, 2011.

13. William C. Mann, "Pace: Troops Must Prevent Iraqi Abuse," Associated Press, November 30, 2005.

14. Denver Nicks, "Private Manning and the Making of Wikileaks," *This Land Press*, September 23, 2010.

15. Manning–Lamo chat logs, available at Wired.com.

16. David Leigh and Maggie O'Kane, "Iraq War Logs: US Turned Over Captives to Iraqi Torture Squads," *Guardian*, October 24, 2010.

Chapter 2. The Life of Bradley Manning

1. Maggie O'Kane, Chavala Madlena and Guy Grandjean, "Bradley Manning: The Bullied Outsider Who Knew US Military's Inner Secrets," *Guardian*, May 27, 2011.

2. Denver Nicks, "Private Manning and the Making of Wikileaks," *This Land Press*, September 23, 2010.

3. Interview with the author, October 7, 2011.

4. "The End of Secrets," transcription of a panel discussion, in *The Law School*, 2011, 22.

5. "Dick Marty Rendition Report Condemns 'Cult of Secrecy,'" *BBC News*, September 7, 2011; James Walsh, "Nobel Peace Prize: Bradley Manning Tops Reader Poll," *Guardian*, October 6, 2011.

6. Nicks, "Private Manning and the Making of Wikileaks."

7. Angie Debo, *And Still the Waters Run: The Betrayal of the Five Civilized Tribes*, Princeton, NJ: Princeton University Press, 1940.

8. Ellen Nakashima, "Bradley Manning Is at the Center of the Wikileaks Controversy. But Who Is He?" *Washington Post*, May 4, 2011.

9. Nicks, "Private Manning and the Making of Wikileaks."

10. Nakashima, "Bradley Manning Is at the Center of the Wikileaks Controversy."

11. Steve Fishman, "Bradley Manning's Army of One," *New York*, July 13, 2011.

12. "Wikileaks: Bradley Manning 'Set Up Own Facebook,'" *Channel 4 News*, December 1, 2010.

13. Nicks, "Private Manning and the Making of Wikileaks."

14. Fishman, "Bradley Manning's Army of One."

15. "The Private Life of Bradley Manning," *Frontline*, broadcast March 29, 2011 on WGBH, Boston.

16. Peter Van Buren, *We Meant Well: How I Helped Lose the Battle for the Hearts and Minds of the Iraqi People*, New York: Metropolitan, 2011, 38.

17. Maggie O'Kane, Chavala Madlena and Guy Grandjean, "Bradley Manning: Fellow Soldier Recalls 'Scared, Bullied Kid,'" *Guardian*, May 28, 2011.

18. Ibid.

19. Ed Pilkington, "Bradley Manning's Internet Chats with Zach Antolak—the Full Text," *Guardian*, July 6, 2011.

20. Maggie O'Kane, Chavala Madlena and Guy Grandjean, "Bradley Manning: The Bullied Outsider Who Knew US Military's Inner Secrets," *Guardian*, May 27, 2011.

21. Interview with the author, October 7, 2011.

22. Maggie O'Kane, Chavala Madlena and Guy Grandjean, "Bradley Manning: The Bullied Outsider."

23. Interview with the author, October 7, 2011.

24. Kevin Poulsen, "Ex-Hacker Adrian Lamo Institutionalized, Diagnosed with Asperger's," *Wired*, May 20, 2010.

25. Gabriel Beltrone, "Mike Huckabee: Leaker Should be Executed," *Politico*, November 30, 2010.

26. Ed Pilkington, "Bradley Manning's Lawyer Demands Sentence Cut," *Guardian*, September 3, 2012.

27. "Bradley Manning Wins Support from Welsh MP and Friends," *BBC News*, March 19, 2011.

28. German Bundestag, "Menschenrechtsausschuss protestiert gegen Haftbedingungen von Bradley Manning," press release issued April 13, 2011.

29. Ed Pilkington, "PJ Crowley Resigns over Bradley Manning Remarks," *Guardian*, March 13, 2011.

30. James Oliphant, "Protest over Accused WikiLeaker Disrupts Obama Fundraiser," *Los Angeles Times*, April 21, 2011.

31. Ellen Nakashima, "Wikileaks: Who is Bradley Manning?" *Washington Post* Live Q&As, May 9, 2011.

32. Joy Reid, "The Manning Chat Logs: TMI and Corroboration of Guilt," *The Reid Report*, July 14, 2011.

33. Greg Mitchell, "Ethan McCord on 'New York' Magazine Profile of Manning: It 'Erases' His Political Motives," *Nation*, July 10, 2011.

34. Interview with the author, August 23, 2011.

Chapter 3. The Leaks

1. *2011 Report to the President*, Washington DC: Information Security Oversight Office, 2011.

2. Steven Aftergood, "NSA Declassifies 200 Year Old Report," *Secrecy News*, June 9, 2011.

3. Mimi Whitefield, "CIA Declassifies More Bay of Pigs Documents," *Miami Herald*, August 15, 2011.

4. Elizabeth Goitein and David M. Shapiro, *Reducing Overclassification Through Accountability*, New York: Brennan Center for Justice, 2011.

5. Coleen Rowley and Bogdan Dzakovic, "Wikileaks and 9/11: What If?" *Los Angeles Times*, October 15, 2010.

6. Scott Shane, "Complaint Seeks Punishment for Overclassification of Documents," *New York Times*, August 1, 2011.

7. Steven Aftergood, "Fundamental Review Yields Reduction in Scope of Secrecy," *Secrecy News*, October 3, 2011.

8. Shane, "Complaint Seeks Punishment for Overclassification of Documents."

9. Glenn Greenwald, "Secrecy, Leaks and the Real Criminals," *Salon*, August 26, 2011.

10. Ibid.

11. Claire Suddath, "How Not to Censor a Book: Pentagon Makes a Best Seller," *Time*, September 30, 2010.

12. Ibid.

13. Shane, "Complaint Seeks Punishment for Overclassification of Documents."

14. Scott Shane, "No Jail Time in Trial over N.S.A. Leak," *New York Times*, July 15, 2011.

15. Elisabeth Bumiller, "Gates on Leaks, Wiki and Otherwise," *New York Times*, November 30, 2010.

16. Glenn Greenwald, "Urgent Leak Investigation Needed," *Salon*, March 24, 2011.

17. Benjamin Wittes, "'I'm All for Leaking When It's Organized,'" *Lawfare*, October 29, 2011.

18. Dana Priest and William M. Arkin, *Top Secret America: The Rise of the New American Security State*, New York: Little Brown, 2011, 26.

19. Ibid., 263–5.

20. Ibid., 264.

21. Ibid., 24.

22. Will Graff, "Manning Peer Sheds Light on Wikileaks: Former Military Intel Analyst Shares His Thoughts on the Motive of Alleged Leaks," *Western Front Online*, April 15, 2011.

23. Ibid.

24. Nick Davies, "Afghanistan War Logs: Task Force 373—Special Forces Hunting Top Taliban," *Guardian*, July 25, 2010.

25. C. J. Chivers, "Strategic Plans Spawned Bitter End for a Lonely Outpost," *New York Times*, July 25, 2010.

26. Nick Davies and David Leigh, "Massive Leak of Secret Files Exposes Truth of Occupation," *Guardian*, July 25, 2010.

27. Declan Walsh, "Afghanistan War Logs: White House Attacks Pakistan over Taliban Aid," *Guardian*, July 25, 2010.

28. www.collateralmurder.com.

29. David Harrison, "Wikileaks: Civilians Gunned Down at Checkpoints," *Telegraph*, October 23, 2010.

30. Matthew Schofield, "Wikileaks: Iraqi Children in U.S. Raid Shot In Head," *Toronto Star*, August 31, 2011.

31. "Huge Wikileaks Release Shows US 'Ignored Iraq Torture,' *BBC News*, October 23, 2010.

32. Glenn Greenwald, "Newly Leaked Documents Show the Ongoing Travesty of Guantánamo," *Salon*, April 25, 2011.

33. James Ball, "Guantánamo Bay Files: Anti-Extremist Author Framed and Whisked to Cuba," *Guardian*, April 24, 2011.

34. Razeshta Sethna, "Pakistani Prisoners at Bagram Wait for Justice," *Dawn*, December 4, 2011.

35. "After Wikileaks Scolding, Top Offical Says Excess Vice Ministers Are Out," *Dominican Today*, September 19, 2011.

36. Emile Mervin, "The People of Guyana Have to Be Grateful for the Wikileaks Cables," *Stabroek News*, September 15, 2011.

37. Scott Horton, "The El-Masri Cable," *Harper's*, November 29, 2010.

38. Gianluca Di Feo and Stefania Maurizi, "Objective: Enlist Wojtyla," *L'Espresso*, April 22, 2011.

39. Julian Borger, "Obama Administration 'Supplied Bunker-Busting Bombs to Israel,'" *The Guardian*, September 27, 2011.

40. "Wikileaks: Israel Aimed to Keep Gaza Economy on Brink of Collapse," *Haaretz*, May 1, 2011.

41. US State Department cable 10TELAVIV182, January 27, 2010.

42. Dan Coughlin and Kim Ives, "Wikileaks Haiti: Let Them Live on $3 a Day," *Nation*, June 1, 2011.

43. James Love, "Looking at Wikileaks Cables on Pharmaceutical Drugs and Trade Pressures," *Le Monde Diplomatique*, September 2011.

44. Michelle Frey, "New Wikileaks Revelations Shed Light on Arctic Oil 'Carve-Up,'" Greenpeace blog, May 12, 2011.

45. Jack Shafer, "Wikileaks, Hillary Clinton, and the Smoking Gun," *Slate*, November 29, 2010.

46. Nancy A. Youseff, "Officials May Be Overstating the Danger from Wikileaks," *McClatchy*, November 28, 2010.

47. "George Packer on Wikileaks and Julian Assange," *The Brian Lehrer Show*, December 7, 2010.

48. Mark Clayton, "Wikileaks List of 'Critical' Sites: Is It a 'Menu for Terrorists'?" *Christian Science Monitor*, December 6, 2010.

49. Bradley Klapper and Cassandra Vinograd, "AP Review Finds No Threatened Wikileaks Sources," *Associated Press*, September 10, 2011.

50. Peter Ford, "No Retribution for Wikileaks Outing Chinese Sources," *Christian Science Monitor*, September 13, 2011.

51. Jeffrey Goldberg, "Wikileaks Scores Again," *The Atlantic* online, October 10, 2011.

52. David van Biema, "The Last Jews of Baghdad," *Time*, July 27, 2007.

53. "Dick Marty Rendition Report Condemns 'Cult of Secrecy,'" *BBC News*, September 7, 2011.

Chapter 4. Whistleblowers and Their Public

1. David Corn, "Colin Powell's Vietnam Fog," *Nation*, May 14, 2001.

2. Alexander Cockburn, "Julian Assange: Wanted by the Empire, Dead or Alive," *Counterpunch*, December 3–5, 2010.

3. John Cary Sims, "Triangulating the Boundaries of the Pentagon Papers," *William & Mary Bill of Rights Journal* 2:2, 1993, 341.

4. Sanford J. Unger, *The Papers and the Papers: An Account of the Legal and Political Battle over the Pentagon Papers*, New York: Dutton, 1972, 302.

5. Alexander Cockburn, "Do Disclosures of Atrocities Change Anything?" *Counterpunch*, July 31–August 2, 2010.

6. Eric Schmitt, "U.S. Envoy's Cables Show Worries on Afghan Plans," *New York Times*, January 25, 2010.

7. Michael White and Brian Whitaker, "UK War Dossier a Sham, Experts Say," *Guardian*, February 7, 2003.

8. Daniel Ellsberg, *Secrets: A Memoir of Vietnam and the Pentagon Papers*, New York: Penguin, 2002, 200–3.

9. Ray McGovern, "Israel's Window to Bomb Iran," *Truthout*, October 4, 2011.

10. Ray McGovern, "An Award or Wikileaks," Antiwar.com, October 25, 2010.

11. Ray McGovern, "Standing Up To War and Hillary Clinton," *Consortium News*, February 23, 2011.

12. Interview with the author, August 19, 2011.

13. Claude Fischer, "Sweet Land of ... Conformity?" *Boston Globe*, June 6, 2010.

Chapter 5. The Torture of Bradley Manning

1. Adrian Lamo, panel discussion at HOPE Conference, New York, July 20, 2010, available at archive.org.

2. *The Istanbul Statement on the Use and Effects of Solitary Confinement*, adopted on December 9, 2007, at the International Psychological Trauma Symposium, Istanbul.

3. Jules Lobel, "Prolonged Solitary Confinement and the Constitution," *University of Pennsylvania Journal of Constitutional Law*, 11:1, 2008, 124.

4. Andy Worthington, "Is Bradley Manning Being Held as Some Sort of 'Enemy Combatant'?" AndyWorthington.co.uk, December 20, 2010.

5. Lisa Hajjar, "Pvt Manning Proves Slippery Slope," *Al Jazeera*, March 15, 2011.

6. *Graham v. Florida*, 130 S. Ct. at 2030.

7. Thomas Geoghegan, *In America's Court: How a Civil Lawyer Who Likes to Settle Stumbled into a Criminal Trial*, New York: New Press, 2003.

8. Nicholas Confessore, "New York Finds Extreme Crisis in Youth Prisons," *New York Times*, December 13, 2009.

9. Interview with the author, May 31, 2010.

10. Interview with the author, May 12, 2010.

11. Jack Dolan, "Indefinite Solitary Confinement Persists in California Prisons," *Los Angeles Times*, September 5, 2011.

12. James Ridgeway and Jean Casella, "The Lonely Battle Against Solitary Confinement," *Guardian*, January 19, 2011.

13. Lobel, "Prolonged Solitary Confinement and the Constitution," 118.

14. *In re Medley*, 134 U.S. 160, 168 (1890).

15. See Margaret Kimberley, "Peace Prize Torture," *Black Agenda Report*, March 19, 2011; Bob Herbert, "America's Abu Ghraibs," *New York Times*, May 31, 2004; James Forman, Jr., "Exporting Harshness," 33; *N.Y.U. Review of Law and Social Change* 33, 2009, 331–74.

16. Jared Ball, "Bradley Manning, Political Imprisonment and the Myopia of the Left," *Black Agenda Report*, July 13, 2011.

17. Atul Gawande, "Hellhole," *New Yorker*, March 30, 2009.

18. Jean Casella and James Ridgeway, "The End of Mississippi's Notorious SuperMax Unit," *Solitary Watch*, June 12, 2010.

19. Gawande, "Hellhole."

20. Ian Lovett, "Hunger Strike by Inmates Is Latest Challenge to California's Prison System," *New York Times*, July 7, 2011.

21. Dolan, "Indefinite Solitary Confinement Persists in California Prisons."

22. Erica Goode, "Prisoners Renew a Protest in California," *New York Times*, September 30, 2011.

Chapter 6. The Rule of Law and Bradley Manning

1. Melissa Harris-Perry, "The Torture Photos," *Nation*, May 14, 2009.

2. Colleen Curry, "Marine's Light Sentence for Iraqi Deaths Sparks Anger," *ABC News*, January 25, 2012.

3. Greg Mitchell, "Ethan McCord on 'New York' Magazine Profile of Bradley Manning: It 'Erases' His Political Motives," *Nation*, July 10, 2011.

4. Scott Horton, "The Law of Armed Conflict: Six Questions for Gary Solis," *Harper's*, April 20, 2010.

5. Nick Davies, "Iraq War Logs: Secret Order That Let US Ignore Abuse," *Guardian*, October 22, 2010.

6. David Kennedy, *Of War and Law*, Princeton, 2006, 167.

7. Frédéric Mégret, "From 'Savages' to 'Unlawful Combatants': A Postcolonial Look at International Humanitarian Law's 'Other,'" *International Law and its 'Others,'* ed. Anne Orford, Cambridge: Cambridge University Press, 2006.

8. Karma Nabulsi, *Traditions of War*, Oxford, 1999, 129.

9. Conor Gearty, "Short Cuts," *London Review of Books*, September 8, 2011.

10. Adrian Vermeule, "Our Schmittian Administrative Law," *Harvard Law Review* 122, 2009, 1095–149.

Chapter 7. The Court-Martial of Bradley Manning

1. Ben Wizner, "The Government's Overreach on Bradley Manning," ACLU Blog of Rights, April 26, 2012.

2. Dana Priest and William M. Arkin, *Top Secret America: The Rise of the New American Security State*, New York: Little Brown, 2011, 58.

3. Zinnia Jones, "Manning Trial: Being Transgender Doesn't Mean You're Unstable," *Huffington Post*, December 6, 2012.

4. "Transgender Need Not Apply: A Report on Gender Identity Job Discrimination," Make the Road New York, March 2010, available online.

5. Tom Cohen, "Congressional Leaders Call for Halt to 'Cascade of Leaks'," CNN, June 7, 2012.

6. Ed Pilkington, "US Government's Handling of State Secrets Is 'Outmoded', Says Report," *Guardian*, December 6, 2012.

7. CNN Wire Staff, "Assange Attorney: Secret Grand Jury Meeting in Virginia on Wikileaks," December 13, 2010.

8. Philip Dorling, "US Calls Assange 'Enemy of State'," *Sydney Morning Herald*, September 27, 2012.

9. "Sweden Violated Torture Ban in CIA Rendition," Human Rights Watch, November 10, 2006.

10. Jesselyn Radack, "What the New York Times Missed in Its 1st Article on Manning's Torture Hearing," *Daily Kos*, December 8, 2012.

11. Ed Pilkington, "Wikileaks Suspect Manning Mistreated by Military, Psychiatrist Says," *Guardian*, November 28, 2012.

12. The following paragraphs are based on courtside reporting done by Nathan Fuller, Bradley Manning Support Network; Kevin Gosztola, FireDogLake's Dissenter blog; and Ed Pilkington's reporting in the *Guardian*.

13. Eliza Gray, "Manning Gets No Love from the New York Times," *New Republic*, December 5, 2012.

ACKNOWLEDGMENTS

First, thanks to Tom Engelhardt, editor of TomDispatch, for putting me on this story to begin with and for his enthusiasm and sage counsel throughout.

Jesselyn Radack, National Security and Human Rights Director of the Government Accountability Office, gave me a detailed tutorial on whistleblower protection law, laws in which she has figured heroically as both attorney and client. Professor Marjorie Cohn of the Thomas Jefferson School of Law graciously shared her expertise on conscientious objector cases and Susan Tipograph of the New York chapter of the National Lawyers Guild, gave of her treasure-house of courtroom war stories to tell me about political defenses.

Many thanks to Steven Aftergood of the Federation of American Scientists for giving his expert opinion on over-classification and on Wikileaks.

Dr. Larbi Sadiki of the University of Exeter and Al Jazeera and Jillian York of the Electronic Frontier Foundation both gave me thoughtful, invaluable insight into the role Wikileaks did and did not play in the Tunisian uprising and the Arab Spring more generally.

Ray McGovern, retired senior analyst for CIA, generously gave of his wisdom and knowledge and a riveting seminar in Thomist political philosophy.

Thanks to Kim Ives of Haiti Liberté for introducing me to Haitian-American leaders like the great Tony Jean-Thenor, who told me how the Haiti leaks had energized his community group.

Historians John Milton Cooper of the University of Wisconsin at Madison and Trygve Thronveit of Harvard put Wilson's notion of "open diplomacy" in proper historical perspective. My great mentor Bart Bernstein, Professor Emeritus of History at Stanford, provided many connections and a candid account of the way Washington over-classifies diplomatic records.

Thanks to Chavala Madlena, Maggie O'Kane and Guy Grandjean of *The Guardian* for sharing a source with me, and for their unsurpassed reporting on Bradley Manning's time in the US Army.

Jacob Sullivan and Peter Van Buren both told me about their time on FOB Hammer in the Mada'in Qada desert of Iraq. Van Buren's rich and scabrous memoir of his stint as a Foreign Service Officer in Iraq, *We Meant Well* (Metropolitan, 2011), is and will continue to be one of the best books on the US invasion and occupation.

Bryan Stevenson, Equal Justice Initiative, gave of his valuable time to discuss the numerous "black holes" in our everyday domestic legal system; Jean Casella and James Ridgeway of the excellent Solitary Watch also gave me friendly help.

Many thanks to David Glazier of Loyola Law School and Michelle McCluer, Executive Director of the National Institute of Military Justice at the Washington College of Law, who were a constant source of rapid elucidation on military law and procedure.

I owe tuition to Naz Modirzadeh, Associate Director of Harvard's Program on Humanitarian Policy and Conflict Research for the excellent backgrounder she gave me on the laws of armed conflict; thanks also to Claude Bruderlein, Executive Director of the Program, for the thoughtful comments he provided. Thank you to Gabor Rona, Legal Director of Human Rights First and Tom Parker, Policy Director for Terrorism, Counterterrorism and Human Rights at Amnesty International for their thoughts on the "Collateral Murder" video and the laws of armed conflict. Thanks also to Gary Solis of Georgetown University Law Center for a long interview on international humanitarian law.

Scholars Peter S. Cahn and Florian Schui supplied valuable leads about Oklahoma's radical heritage and Enlightenment thought on government secrecy, respectively. Charlie Davis blew the whistle on the high-minded liberal betrayal of Bradley Manning.

I am indebted to my publisher, John Oakes and to the OR Books team of Fernanda Diaz and Crystal Williams for their patience and hard work, and to my friend Graydon Gordian for seeing through the first phase of the project. Thanks to Tom Tomorrow for granting permission to use his splendid cartoons.

Thanks to Rich Chang for edits on the biographical section, and to my brother Josiah Madar for a deep reading and the rule of law chapter.

Thanks to Amanda and Bill Madar who obliged their firstborn by converting their home into a deluxe writer's colony for nearly a month.

Eyal Press, Nicholas Arons, Belén Fernández, Idrees Ahmad, Adam Shatz, Karma Nabulsi, Satish Moorthy and Troy Selvaratnam all fueled the project with their unsolicited encouragement. I am grateful for an emergency power boost from Rosemond and Nils Vaule and for a neighborly landline from Lumi Rolley and Eric McClure.

Most of all, thanks to my luminous bride Jennifer M. Turner for her love and care and edits *and* supreme patience throughout.

FOR FURTHER READING

The story of Pfc. Manning is not over; this book is likely only the first installment.

For updates on his case and on the movement behind him, the best source is the Bradley Manning Support Network website, www.bradleymanning. org. Kevin Gosztola of FireDogLake's "Dissenter" blog has provided excellent up-to-the-minute coverage, and his FDL colleagues Marcy Wheeler and Jane Hamsher have also poured their talent and energy into thoughtful analyses. Glenn Greenwald at *The Guardian* newspaper has also brought his skills as a constitutional lawyer and fiercely independent mind to bear on all the issues at stake in this case. The various Wikileaks sites—Wikileaks Press and Wikileaks Central, among others—also provide constant news and updates. (Traditional print media has not been wholly deficient: *The Guardian* has covered the Manning story with a thoroughness and sense of proportion rarely found in other newspapers.)

Manning's lawyer, David E. Coombs, gives valuable regular updates on his blog and website, www.armycourtmartialdefense.com.

For news on over-classification and government secrecy, Steven Aftergood of the Federation of American Scientists blogs regularly while the National Security Archive focuses on the declassification of foreign policy documents.

Stay current on the overuse of solitary confinement in America and the struggle to end it at the websites of Solitary Watch and the National Religious Campaign Against Torture. For coverage of Guantánamo and other war on terror detention matters, no one surpasses author, reporter and blogger Andy Worthington. Anything by Carol Rosenberg of the Miami *Herald*, the dean of Gitmo journalists who has been whisked off the base once and banned a second time, is also well worth reading.

For foreign affairs coverage outside the narrow Beltway consensus, the first step is to subscribe to TomDispatch's thrice-weekly reports. CounterPunch and PulseMedia provide a variety of left-of-center viewpoints; *The American Conservative* provides an equally anti-imperialist outlook from the paleoconservative right. (Daniel Larison's Eunomia blog at the TAC site is particularly worthwhile.) Black Agenda Report examines Washington and the world from a Black left perspective and is essential reading. Critical views from the "realist" school can be found at Stephen Walt's excellent ForeignPolicy.com blog, also on the terrific group blog "The Skeptics" at The National Interest. Electronic Intifada and MondoWeiss offer badly needed analysis and opinions on US policy in the Middle East, as does Al Jazeera's English website. AntiWar.com, run by libertarians but politically ecumenical, is a daily must.

The greatest source of critical views on international law and the laws of war is the Italian site Jura Gentium run by Professor Danilo Zolo at the University of Florence. Much of it is translated into English.

As of this writing, Pfc. Bradley Manning himself can be reached at Commander, HHC USAG/ATTN: PFC Manning/239 Sheridan Avenue, Bldg 417/JBM-HH, VA 22211. According to his lawyer, Bradley Manning greatly appreciates friendly letters.